# DOG TRAINING

## The Essential Guide

Lisa
Tenzin-Dolma

*Dog Training: The Essential Guide* is also available in accessible formats for people with any degree of visual impairment. The large print edition and e-book (with accessibility features enabled) are available from Need2Know. Please let us know if there are any special features you require and we will do our best to accommodate your needs.

First published in Great Britain in 2012 by
Need2Know
Remus House
Coltsfoot Drive
Peterborough
PE2 9BF
Telephone 01733 898103
Fax 01733 313524
www.need2knowbooks.co.uk

# Contents

# Introduction

A dog who greets people and other dogs politely, who comes when you call him, and who is well behaved when left to his own devices, is a joy to have around. Along with the pleasure of companionship and the prospect of experiencing the unconditional love and devotion that dogs give so freely, this is the ideal image that most people have in their minds when considering bringing home a puppy or rescue dog.

Yet often the reality can be very different. A pooch who mugs visitors as they come through the door, who employs selective deafness when called, who wrecks the home when left alone, or who greets other dogs by hurling himself playfully at them or displaying aggression can make you wonder why you ever wanted a dog in your life. If you get off to the right start these behaviours won't occur, because your dog will understand what is expected of him and will be happy to cooperate with you.

Teaching your dog basic training is the key to responsible dog ownership. It keeps him (and other dogs and people) safe and at ease, and it fosters strong bonds of affection and respect between you and your dog. Training your dog should be fun, and making it into a game speeds up his learning processes. It builds a foundation of mutual trust and rapport and gives both of you a feeling of wellbeing. It also means that you can relax and enjoy your dog's company – which is most likely the main reason why you decided to share your life and your home with a furry friend.

From the moment you bring your dog home, you take on the role of teacher and guide. If your dog is a puppy, he will have been strongly influenced by the environment in which he spent his first few weeks. Because of this, it's important to see him with his mother and littermates. If the mother is friendly and your pup has already been introduced to people, he will arrive with an attitude that new experiences are exciting, rather than scary. If his start in life hasn't been good, you may have to initially put extra effort into helping him relax and settle in. If you have adopted a rescue dog, his background may not be known. He may have experienced hardship, abuse, neglect or hunger. Yet

'Teaching your dog basic training is the key to responsible dog ownership.'

dogs are extraordinarily forgiving and they live very much in the moment, so kindness and understanding will quickly earn you the trust of a dog of any age or background.

With dogs, as with people, the most effective teaching occurs when you allow them to work things out for themselves through calm, patient, gentle guidance. Once a dog understands what you're asking of him and realises that good things happen when he complies, he'll be your willing student. This is why reward-based training, also called positive reinforcement, works best.

Until recently, the methods used in dog training were based on punishment for lack of cooperation. The idea behind this was that dogs needed to know who was boss (you). Otherwise, if given the chance, they would rule the roost. The 'dominance' methods, which sadly are still in use in some quarters, are based on the idea that dogs retain the characteristics of their distant ancestors, wolves, that they operate according to a hierarchical system, and that they will make every effort to reach (and stay on) the top rung of the hierarchical ladder.

'With dogs, as with people, the most effective teaching occurs when you allow them to work things out for themselves through calm, patient, gentle guidance.'

A great deal of scientific research has been done into this, and the dominance theory has now been disproved. Recent research has shown that dogs are social creatures who have evolved alongside humans for many thousands of years, and whose brains have been hardwired, as a result of this, to relate even more closely to humans than to other dogs. Dogs view us as their companions, even as family, and they respond best to kindness and to being rewarded for desirable behaviour rather than punished for undesirable behaviour.

Your role as teacher is to guide your dog towards displaying the behaviour you want from him. If your dog 'gets' what you're asking of him, and complies, immediately giving him rewards in the form of praise, a food treat or a game will help to fix his response to your instructions so that he remembers what to do in the future. Through practice, you are effectively creating a habit that he will always follow through on.

If your dog isn't cooperating, ask yourself why this could be. Perhaps you're not being clear enough, and he doesn't understand what you want from him. Perhaps you told him off, or looked disapproving, when he didn't come up with the asked-for response. Or perhaps you rewarded him too late when he did as you asked. Dogs have short memories for associations while they're learning something new, so it's important to reward him immediately so that he realises exactly what he's done right.

Dogs don't learn effectively if they're punished when they have done something wrong. This makes them confused and fearful, and dogs will mentally 'shut down' when they're scared, so find it much harder to learn. When you use positive reinforcement, this makes your dog a willing and eager pupil who looks to you for guidance and confirmation.

Positive methods also involve setting and keeping rules. Dogs, like children, need guidelines and boundaries, so that they understand what is acceptable and what isn't. Think about which rules are most important to you, and keep these to a minimum so that you can follow through on them. If you have too many rules and regulations, your life with your dog will be too regimented to be as enjoyable as it could be and it's more likely that rules will be broken.

Your rules might include greeting visitors politely, coming when called, keeping a reasonable distance during your mealtimes, and staying off the sofa (or getting off when you want to sit down). Perhaps there are other things which are important to you, but do try to ensure that any rules you have will be consistently enforced. If you want your dog to learn table manners, but your dog is fed scraps from your plate one day and told off for begging another day, he won't understand why he's in trouble and will keep on asking for a morsel of your meal.

'Your role as teacher is to guide your dog towards displaying the behaviour you want from him.'

The company of a dog can add a new dimension to life. When the relationship is built on trust and understanding, it can be immensely rewarding for you as well as for your dog. Dogs open our hearts, make us laugh, uplift us with their company even during difficult times. Having glimpses into the mind of a dog brings about a sense of respect for these creatures from another species who willingly choose to be with us and learn from us. Training your dog will be a journey of discovery for both of you, and this book aims to help you find the path where footprints and pawprints can walk side by side, in harmony.

Throughout this book I have referred to dogs in the masculine for ease of reading, simply because I have two male dogs. If your dog is female, please substitute 'she' for 'he'.

## Acknowledgements

Many thanks to Amy Sutcliffe at Need2Know Books, for her enthusiasm over this book, and to my talented daughter, Amber Tenzin-Dolma, for the photo illustrations. Thanks also to the owners who allowed us to photograph their dogs for this book: Shirley and Geoff, with Toes and Tara; Pam, Paul and James, with Cyder; Sue and Graham, with Rosie; and Angie and Pete, with Maisie.

'Positive methods also involve setting and keeping rules.'

Cyder

Duke

8

Maisie

Rosie

Skye

'The company of
a dog can add a
new dimension
to life.'

Toes and Tara

My clients and their dogs have taught me so much over the years; and my students at The International School of Canine Psychology ask me such good questions (and provide excellent answers of their own) during our group discussions. Much gratitude is also due to the members of Oldies Club dog rescue charity and to my fellow members of The Association of INTO Dogs – especially Theo Stewart, chair of INTO Dogs, for test-reading this book and giving valuable feedback. I'm forever indebted to my own dogs and foster dogs, those four-legged mentors and playmates who have always been my daily guides into the workings of the ever-fascinating canine mind. Thanks always to my own dogs who appear in the photos in this book: our beloved Duke Greyhound, who passed away soon after this book was completed; and my constant companion and dear friend Skye Lurcher, who is such a wise mentor and guide to all my foster dogs.

## Disclaimer

This book is for general information on dog training, and isn't intended to replace professional behavioural and training advice. If you are experiencing issues with your dog, it is important that you consult with a behaviourist or trainer who uses positive methods.

# Chapter One

# Positive Reinforcement

Dogs repeat behaviours that they find rewarding in some way, even if what a dog views as rewarding may not make sense to us. For instance, compulsive licking can make a dog's skin very sore, yet the reward gained for the dog is the release of endorphins (pleasure-inducing chemicals) that ease feelings of stress or anxiety. If your dog is misbehaving and you tell him off, the reward he gains from being chastised is your attention – and any attention, to your dog's mind, may be a bonus, so he'll gaily continue to do whatever it is that you are trying to prevent him from doing. Because dogs respond best to a feedback response that brings a promise of reward, the positive training methods work far better than fear-inducing punishment. Reward-based training is the perfect way to teach your dog to focus on you. It increases trust, and results in much happier dogs and owners.

'Dogs repeat behaviours that they find rewarding in some way.'

## What is positive reinforcement?

Positive reinforcement is the act of rewarding your dog with praise, a food treat, a toy or a game as soon as he follows through on the behaviour that you want from him. You need to be quick off the mark when you acknowledge the desirable behaviour, because otherwise you may inadvertently create a connection in your dog's mind between the reward and something else that he has just done. A space of no more than two seconds between action and reward works best.

Say you're teaching your dog to sit, and he sits beautifully for a moment. You say 'sit' as his rear end touches the floor and he stands as you give him the reward. The connection made in your dog's mind will be that he gets rewarded for standing, so make sure that you give the praise and reward as he sits, not when he's changed position. Timing is everything!

When you use reward-based training, you are tapping into your dog's psyche and instinctive nature. As any behaviour that results in making your dog feel good will consequently be repeated, positive reinforcement ensures that your dog gets into the habit of following through on the desirable behaviours that you are teaching him.

## Which rewards can you use?

Attention is almost always viewed by your dog as a reward. Some dogs are 'foodies' and will do anything you ask of them if there's the prospect of a tasty treat. Some dogs aren't particularly interested in food, but are passionate about a specific toy. Other dogs light up if they're rewarded with a game, such as tug or retrieve. You can experiment to find out what works best with your dog.

'Attention is almost always viewed by your dog as a reward.'

The chosen reward should be forthcoming every time your dog does as he's asked, until this becomes an ingrained habit. When your dog consistently follows through on instructions, you can gradually reduce the food or game rewards so that they come occasionally, at random. By this time, your dog will be conditioned to give the desired response, but an occasional extra reward will keep him focused on you, as he'll always hope that this time he'll get it. Always give praise, even after you've reduced the amount of rewards, as your approval is a reward in itself.

Food rewards should be deducted from your dog's daily food intake, so that he doesn't become overweight. The treats can be small – a sliver of chicken, a tiny cube of cheese, or a thin slice of sausage work very well, or you may prefer to use good-quality pre-packaged treats.

Remember that when you give a reward you're very effectively saying 'Thank you' to your dog for carrying out the requested behaviour. By saying 'Good boy' or 'Thank you' as you give it, you're acknowledging that you're pleased with him – and dogs love to have a happy owner!

Your dog will find some training tasks harder to figure out than others. Save the best rewards for the responses that your dog finds most difficult. This is called a 'high value' reward. If you're teaching recall but your dog is distracted by another person or dog and won't come when you call him, remember that, for him, the reward of different company is more enticing (high value) than the same old treat that you always give him. Have something different in your pocket for these occasions, so that your reward is more appealing to him.

## What is negative reinforcement?

Negative reinforcement was a major aspect in dog training until it was proven that reward-based methods work best. Negative reinforcement involves causing discomfort to the dog so that he learns that this behaviour has unpleasant or painful consequences. Using the old, harsh methods, a dog was taught to walk to heel by 'correcting' the dog, through jerking hard and fast on the lead as soon as he moved away from his owner's side. This hurt the dog's sensitive neck and throat. Eventually, the theory goes, he would associate moving away with the experience of pain and would learn to stay close beside his owner in order to avoid further discomfort. However, when this is done most dogs tend to try to pull harder to create more distance between themselves and the cause of the pain (the owner!). Positive dog training methods steer well clear of the use of negative reinforcement.

## What is conditioning?

Every experience your dog undergoes brings some of form of teaching and may be viewed as positive or negative by your dog. From birth, your dog's experiences condition his mind to work in a certain way, which is why it's important that dogs have many positive experiences during the first few weeks. The conditioning he receives as a puppy will influence his behaviour as an adult dog; and the conditioning he receives from you, throughout his life, determines how he learns to respond to different stimuli and whether he views the world as a good or hostile place. The methods you use for training your dog effectively condition him – they set him up to repeat a desired response.

Conditioning is the term used for how your dog's outlook, expectations and responses are shaped. There are two forms of this: classical conditioning and operant conditioning.

'Save the best rewards for the responses that your dog finds most difficult.'

## Classical conditioning

Classical conditioning, also called respondent conditioning, involves bringing about a predictable response that the dog has no control over. The most famous example is that of Pavlov's dogs. In the early 1900s, scientist Ivan Petrovich Pavlov was conducting experiments in analysing dogs' saliva. He discovered that if he rang a bell and immediately gave food to the dogs, they began to salivate as soon as they heard the bell ring, even when no food was given. The dogs quickly learned to associate the sound of the bell with food and their bodies couldn't help but respond, even when no food appeared.

## Operant conditioning

Operant conditioning, also called instrumental conditioning, is the system most used in positive dog training. It works on the premise that any behaviour that the dog finds rewarding will be repeated, thereby creating a pattern or habit. If a behaviour brings about an unpleasant response, or no response, the dog will cease to repeat that behaviour. In behavioural terms we call this 'extinguishing'. If you reward your dog every time he does as you ask, he will swiftly learn to cooperate. Once his response is consistent, you can gradually reduce or tail off the rewards, but your dog will still repeat the behaviour when you ask him to. He will be exhibiting a conditioned response.

However, this can backfire if you inadvertently reward your dog for an unwanted behaviour. Say your dog is barking at you to demand attention or a game, and you tell him to be quiet, or you set aside what you're doing and play with him – in future, your dog will bark at you, expecting you to concede to his wish for attention. He will have very effectively conditioned you! It's important that you only reward the behaviours that you want your dog to display.

# What is redirection?

Redirection is another method used in dog training – and it can be very useful when your dog is up to something that doesn't meet with your approval. For instance, your dog is busy chewing one of your favourite shoes to shreds. Shouting at him to stop will only get him more excited. Grabbing the shoe will either be viewed by your dog as a great new game of tug, or will make him angry because possession is ten tenths of the law in a dog's mind. Both of these responses are giving your dog a great deal of attention and are likely to lead to the loss of more shoes in future. Redirection is a wiser course of action. Instead of engaging in a game or battle, you can call your dog away from a distance, at the same time offering a chew or a toy which appeals to him. As soon as he takes the reward, you can remove your shoe. His attention has been redirected onto something more appropriate.

## What can you do when your dog pushes the boundaries?

In the introduction it was mentioned that boundaries are important for dogs, just as they are for people. By teaching boundaries you are guiding your dog towards feeling secure, staying safe, keeping others safe, and to learning good manners that will make him a pleasure to be with. Some dogs are generally compliant and easy to teach, while other dogs will strive, like unruly children, to push the boundaries to the limit, leaving you feeling irritated, frustrated or plain exhausted.

Adolescence is the typical time when even the most easy-going dogs tend to test you. This occurs between the ages of around six to eighteen months, and it's no coincidence that it's a common age group for dogs sadly waiting to be rehomed at rescue shelters. That sweet puppy who took to training like the proverbial duck to water suddenly seems to forget what you've taught him and refuses to cooperate.

'Adolescent dogs are rather like teenagers whose hormones are raging and who feel compelled to rebel against authority.'

Adolescent dogs are rather like teenagers whose hormones are raging and who feel compelled to rebel against authority. This isn't a comfortable time for your dog and it's no fun for you, either, if you don't know how to address the changes in his behaviour. Often by this stage his training has appeared to be established, and you're used to having him follow through on instructions, so it can be a shock if he becomes either selectively deaf or openly defiant.

The solution is to stay calm, keep your head, avoid indulging in noisy reactions to his misdemeanours and clearly redefine the boundaries. Keep the rules as simple and straightforward as possible and go back to basics with the training.

It's likely that you haven't needed to give him food or play rewards as often recently, so reintroduce these and give them, with fulsome praise, every single time your dog follows through on your requests.

Punishment or raised voices will only alienate your dog and exacerbate the unwanted behaviour, but if he is overstepping the mark by challenging you or becoming overexcited, the most effective form of discipline is temporary exclusion. Dogs are social creatures. They don't like to feel left out or banished. Calmly removing your dog from the room, with a closed door between you for a minute, certainly no more than two minutes, effectively teaches him that his behaviour has been unacceptable. Please don't do this unless it's absolutely necessary – it's best to focus on positive reinforcement or redirection whenever possible, but brief exclusion is very effective for serious lapses in conduct, as long as this really is brief, because after a couple of minutes your dog will have forgotten why he has been banished.

'It has become accepted by scientists that positive methods work.'

This phase passes quickly if you take steps to retrain your dog as soon as you notice signs of rebellion, especially if you have had the opportunity to bond with your dog. If you have adopted an adult dog, you may find that he displays these tendencies a few weeks after moving in with you, when he's started to feel a bit more secure. He's unpacking his baggage and testing the boundaries, so using reward-based training will teach him to relax and trust you.

## What is the science behind positive methods of dog training?

A great deal of research has been undertaken into whether dogs respond best to reward-based or punishment-based methods. It has become accepted by scientists that positive methods work, and that the old 'dominance' methods are cruel, unconstructive and ineffective.

A number of scientific papers have been published about this. Among these, The Journal of Veterinary Behavior: Clinical Applications and Research published an excellent article in pages 135 to 144 of the May/June issue, 2009, titled *Using 'Dominance' to Explain Dog Behavior is Old Hat*. More recently, in 2012, Prescott Breeden's thoroughly researched article, *Dog Whispering in the*

*20th Century*, which can be found on the Internet, explains in-depth the common misunderstandings about dominance and the reasons why punishment methods don't work.

Scientists have discovered that the emotional bonds between dogs and their owners are extraordinarily powerful. The strength of the love many of us feel for our dogs is similar to that of a parent towards a child and dogs seem to view us almost as parent figures. Dogs are dependent on us for their every need to be met. They rely on us for food, shelter, and to keep them safe, and they thrive when given affection.

Some non-dog owners may baulk at the thought of love between people and dogs, but there is chemical evidence that the bond experienced between people and their dogs is one of love. The chemical is oxytocin, which is often called the 'love hormone' because it floods the systems of both parties when mothers hold and cuddle their babies. Several scientists have engaged in important research into oxytocin levels in people and dogs during affectionate interaction. Among these, Professor Kerstin Uvnäs-Moberg in Sweden discovered that oxytocin levels in the blood of both dogs and their owners were raised when owners stroked their dogs. Miho Nagasawa and Takefumi Kikusui in Japan found that oxytocin levels in urine were raised when dogs and their owners interacted, during play and prolonged eye contact. From a scientific perspective, there is no doubt that a positive, caring relationship between you and your dog creates a bond that may be potentially be as potent as the nurturing of affection between two humans.

# Summing Up

- Dogs repeat behaviours that they find rewarding and reduce or stop behaviours which don't bring a reward.

- Positive reinforcement is the act of rewarding desirable behaviours as soon as they occur.

- Attention, positive or negative, is usually viewed by your dog as a reward.

- Food or play rewards can be gradually reduced once your dog consistently follows through on instructions.

- When you reward your dog with a food treat, toy or game, you are effectively thanking him for doing well.

- Negative reinforcement employs unpleasant or painful corrections and can destroy trust. It is counterproductive to positive dog training.

- Conditioning shapes your dog's outlook, expectations and behaviour.

- Redirection distracts your dog from performing unwanted behaviour.

- Clear boundaries help dogs to know what you expect from them, and help them feel more secure.

- Scientific studies have proven that positive methods work best.

# Chapter Two

# Basic Good Manners

A well-mannered dog is delightful company and a credit to his owner. Learning should be enjoyable and fun for both you and your dog, so the most effective way of teaching your dog good manners is to choose a time when you're both relaxed. Midway between meals is ideal, partly because your dog will be more likely to want to earn food rewards, and partly because dogs need to rest their digestive systems for an hour after mealtimes.

Keep the training sessions short – ten minutes is long enough – so that your dog doesn't lose interest. If your dog seems bored or uncooperative, stop the training session immediately and try again a while later. Try to consistently set your dog up for success, not failure, because a dog who feels he can't get it right for you will soon lose confidence and give up.

Break down each lesson into small increments and proceed at a pace that is comfortable for your dog. Some learn faster than others and some simply need you to be clearer about your guidance, instructions and expectations. A patient approach prevents you from becoming frustrated and disrupting the potential for learning. Most importantly, view this time as special bonding time with your dog. Dogs are highly attuned to our emotions, and they respond best when we're enjoying their company.

'The most effective way of teaching your dog good manners is to choose a time when you're both relaxed.'

## Home and away

In the beginning you may find that your dog responds beautifully at home, but seems to forget his training when you take him out. At home there are less distractions because the environment is familiar, so he'll be more focused on you, whereas out on your walks there are likely to be lots of pulls on his attention. Interesting smells, the presence of other dogs and people, the prospect of a good roll in sweet-smelling grass (or foul-smelling fox poo) may be far more tempting to him than a treat and some praise! If your dog takes a while to do as he's asked during walks, be patient, understand that he's surrounded by other stimuli and always reward him when he does eventually follow through on your requests. If you become frustrated because he's ignoring you, this will change the tone of your voice and will reveal itself through body tension. These subtle signals of displeasure have the effect of making your dog want to move further away from you, or will make him anxious and even less likely to cooperate. Bear in mind that he will learn to respond consistently if you give him time and keep repeating the training until his responses become automatic.

## What's in a name?

'Use his name when you praise him so that he quickly learns to develop a positive association with it.'

It's likely that your dog won't know his name when he first comes to live with you, especially if he's a puppy entering his first home, or a rescue dog who was found lost or abandoned. In these cases, you or the rescue centre will have chosen a name for him.

One common reason why dogs often don't respond to their names, even when they have been in a home for some time, is that the owner uses the name constantly. To the dog's ears it just becomes like white noise that he learns to ignore. Another reason is that the dog's name is always used when he's being reprimanded, so it becomes a signal to move further away instead of closer.

To teach your dog to recognise and respond to his name, make sure that you only use it in a positive sense, and that you always use a happy tone of voice when you say his name.

Call him to you, sounding excited (good things are about to happen!) and reward him with praise and a treat as soon as he responds. Use his name when you praise him ('Good boy, Fido!') so that he quickly learns to develop a positive association with it. Just say his name once each time you use it. If you constantly repeat his name several times, he'll 'tune out'. Imagine how irritated you would feel if someone called you by saying your name over and over!

If your dog has done (or is about to do) something undesirable, such as chewing the rug or preparing to help himself to your meal, use a phrase such as 'Ah ah' or 'Oh oh' instead of his name.

Many dog owners have several pet names as terms of endearment for their dogs. This can be confusing when a dog is first learning his name, so try to stick to the one you have chosen for him.

## Toilet training

Teaching your dog to use the garden as his toilet area is easy when you use a reward-based method. The trick to this is a willingness to go outside with your dog every time you let him outside for a loo break (whatever the weather!), and spot-on timing.

The old methods of using punishment, such as shouting at the dog or even rubbing his nose in the soiled area if he toileted indoors, made toilet training very hard to accomplish. Often the dogs didn't understand why they were being treated roughly and became afraid of their unpredictable owners, or found a hiding place indoors to use as a private toilet.

Your dog can be clean indoors in just a few days when you use positive reinforcement. The number of times you take your dog outside each day while you're training him depends on the age and health of your dog. Puppies have small bladders and need to be taken out every hour or so, as well as after meals, drinks, naps and playtimes. Elderly dogs may need to go out more if their bladders have become weak. Frequent loo breaks are necessary if your dog of any age has a urinary infection. Adult dogs in good health should be taken outside every couple of hours and after drinks, meals, naps and play.

You'll only need to go out this frequently in the short term. After that, you can watch your dog's body language for signs that he needs to 'go'. Sniffing around, circling, pacing, whining or just looking uncomfortable are all signals that tell you your dog needs to eliminate or wee.

Put some treats in your pocket. Call your dog in a bright, cheerful tone of voice and take him outside. The chirpier you sound, the keener he'll be to accompany you. Stand near him, taking care not to loom over him, and let him explore and sniff around. As *soon* as he toilets, drop a treat right in front of his nose and praise him. Use the word that you want him to associate with toileting, such as 'Go wee'. You could then play a game for a minute, if you

'Your dog can be clean indoors in just a few days when you use positive reinforcement.'

like, to create even more positive associations with his outdoor space. After that you can call to him to follow you back indoors. You're helping him learn recall as well as toilet skills if you do this.

A common mistake that people make, even with reward-based methods, is to stand well away from the dog and call him over for his treat after he's toileted. That gives the dog the impression that he's being rewarded for 'coming', instead of for 'going' and makes it harder for him to learn what you're asking of him. Stay close enough to drop the treat *while* he's 'going'.

Even adult dogs who haven't lived indoors usually learn toilet manners in around three days. However, sometimes accidents happen. You may be out of the room, or distracted, so don't notice your dog's signals. Or, if he's a puppy, he may wake up with such a full bladder that he can't get to the door in time. If your dog has an accident, avoid chastising him. Simply take him outside and then come indoors and clean up silently with a product that removes the scent of urine. Biological washing liquid or powder works for this, or you can buy a dedicated product from your local pet shop. Bleach may remove the scent for us, but not for your dog, and if he can smell where he's 'been' before, he may think that's a toilet area and use it again.

Adolescent, unwell or elderly dogs may seem to 'forget' their toilet training. If your dog has been clean indoors but suddenly starts to 'go' inside, it's wise to have him thoroughly checked by your vet, as some health issues can cause loss of bladder or bowel control.

'As *soon* as he toilets, drop a treat right in front of his nose and praise him.'

## Come

It's very important that your dog learns to come to you when you call him. No dog should be allowed out of the garden off-lead until he learns good recall skills. Even dogs with excellent recall may occasionally forget their training if something exciting, such as a squirrel dashing in front of them, occurs. Many of the sad, scared dogs who end up on death row in pounds each year arrive there because they became lost after not returning to their owners when out on walks. If every dog was taught to reliably come to their owners when called, there would also be a much lower incidence of fights and dog attacks.

## Teaching recall skills

Recall skills are easy to teach if you do this in four stages. Start off indoors, where your dog is closer to you and is likely to pay more attention. Gather a handful of small treats and, when your dog is over the other side of the room, call him by name in an excited tone of voice, adding 'Come' immediately after his name. Bend at the waist and tap your thighs or chest if you wish, as dogs respond well to this signal. As soon as your dog comes to you, praise and reward him.

The second stage is to call your dog from another room, so that he's responding just to your voice. Remember to keep your voice upbeat, so that he knows something good is about to happen, and make sure you're delighted to see him as soon as he appears. Praise and reward him.

For the third stage, call him indoors when he's out in the garden, and call him out to the garden when he's indoors. Praise and reward him immediately. By now he'll be conditioned to come to you as soon as you call him. Keep practising, because the more you do this, the faster he'll learn.

The fourth stage takes place while you're out in a safe, enclosed place such as a field or park. Choose a time when there are as few distractions, such as other dogs, as possible. Let him run free, call him, reward him for coming, then clip on his lead for just a few moments before removing his lead and setting him free to play. Repeat this several times. If you only put his lead on when it's time to leave, your dog will soon associate coming to you with the ending of his free running and sniffing around time – and may choose to develop selective deafness if he doesn't want the fun to end. Clipping on his lead and then releasing him again encourages him to come back every time you call him because there's always a reward.

Once you feel confident about your dog's recall skills, you can take him out to busier, more stimulating environments.

The key to consistently good recall is for you to always, *always* be pleased with your dog when he returns to you. If your dog has an off-day, or takes a while to come when you call him, make sure that you still praise him as soon as he arrives beside you. If you get annoyed or frustrated because your dog has

'No dog should be allowed out of the garden off-lead until he learns good recall skills.'

gone galloping in the opposite direction, and you tell him off when he does eventually come back, you'll be teaching him that coming to you equals disapproval or punishment.

Avoid running after him because he'll just view that as a great game and will keep on running away from you. Instead, catch your dog's attention by running in the opposite direction (wave your arms and call excitedly if you like) or simply drop to the ground, crouching and throwing your arms wide open. He'll soon come over to see what's so interesting or exciting. If you chastise your dog when he comes to you, all the energy you previously put into teaching recall will have been wasted – you'll have to start all over again, and work even harder to regain his trust. If you consistently reward him when he comes, after a while he will consistently come when he's called.

'The key to consistently good recall is for you to always, *always* be pleased with your dog when he returns to you.'

## Off-lead manners are important for you, too!

When your dog is off-lead in a public place, please pay close attention to where he is and what he's doing. If you're absorbed in another activity, such as texting or emailing on your mobile phone, or chatting with a friend, you won't see where your dog has gone if he wanders off or goes to investigate an interesting smell or greet another dog. You also won't notice and pick up when he poops, so will be making the walk area unpleasant for other owners.

The consequences of not watching your off-lead dog can be serious. Many of the fights that occur between dogs on walks happen because the owners aren't paying attention and are therefore not in control of the dogs. Children who have been subjected to an overenthusiastic greeting from a strange dog may develop a lifelong fear of dogs as a result of this. Another consideration is that a lot of nasty tummy upsets could be avoided if owners were to stay fully aware of what their dogs are investigating and eating.

## Sit

The old method of teaching a dog to sit was to push down on his rear end and force his bottom to the ground. As dogs resist pressure by moving in the opposite direction, this made it hard for dogs to understand what their trainers wanted from them. Imagine that someone suddenly forcibly puts their hand on you and pushes you into a seated position – your natural impulse would be to try to stay upright and maintain your balance.

Positive training makes learning to sit easy for your dog. There are two methods you can use. The first one takes advantage of the moments when your dog naturally sits of his own accord, so you need to be aware of when he's starting to lower his rear end to the ground. Keep your pocket filled with small treats and say 'Sit' as you treat and praise him every time he happens to sit down. He'll soon make the connection between the word and his action.

The second method involves you choosing when to train your dog. Fill your pocket with small treats, choose a space near a wall, and call your dog over to you, moving slowly and calmly around him until he has plenty of space but his rear end is facing the wall. You can show him a treat to get his attention, if you like. Remember to praise him for coming to you and try not to loom over him, as this will make him feel uncomfortable.

Now hold the treat in your closed hand, with just a bit of the treat poking out. He'll go to sniff or take the treat, but don't give it to him yet. Hold your closed hand near his nose and slowly move it above his head. Your dog's nose will rise up into the air to follow the treat and his rear end will naturally move downwards. Having the wall behind him means that he can't simply step backwards, so will sit down instead. The moment his bottom touches the ground, give the treat and lots of praise.

Keep practising and soon he will understand what you're asking of him, and will be happy to comply. You can then repeat the training in the middle of the room and outdoors.

You can also use a hand signal as a cue for your dog to 'sit'. He'll see this even at a distance. To do this, just put your hand out and raise your wrist so that your fingers move downward.

'Positive training makes learning to sit easy for your dog.'

# Stop

Along with 'Come', this is another of the most important words you can teach your dog. It can avert potential distress or disaster if he's hurtling towards a person or another dog. It can halt him in his tracks if he's about to do something that's forbidden, such as snaffling the biscuits you left within reach. And it can save his life if he sees something interesting by a busy road and is about to dash towards it.

Dogs understand our body language and tones of voice very well, and the 'stop' signal uses both to good effect. You'll be taking a traffic cop as your role model for this. The traffic cop holds out one hand, palm up and outwards, to keep one lane of cars stationary while he uses the other hand to move another lane forward. You'll be using your right hand to stop your dog in his tracks, but you can use both hands if you prefer to.

'Dogs understand our body language and tones of voice very well, and the "stop" signal uses both to good effect.'

Rosie learns the 'stop' signal

The garden is an ideal place to start teaching 'stop'. Somewhere busy, like a park, has too many distractions, whereas your garden is a familiar place and he'll be more likely to give you his full attention.

Wait until your dog is running or sniffing around, then call him to you. As he runs towards you, hold out your hand and say 'Stop' in a firm voice just before he reaches you. Most dogs will immediately stop when you do this, and will pause while they figure out whether to start moving again or stay where they are. As soon as he stops, reward him.

As he learns the principles, you can make this into a fun game for both of you by asking your dog to stop, then calling him to you before sending him on his way and repeating 'stop' as he curves back towards you.

**Need2Know**

You can also use a hand signal as a cue to ask your dog to stop while he's walking beside you. Put your hand by your thighs with your palm facing towards your dog.

## Stop barking!

The 'stop' command also comes in very handy if your dog barks a great deal. Hold out your hand, ask him to 'stop' and say 'Thank you' the moment he pauses to draw breath. Dogs bark in order to get our attention – to let us know there's a noise we should be aware of, or a person or another dog passing too close to their territory. If your dog does this, he genuinely thinks that he's doing you a favour by warning you, so will be confused and puzzled if you react by telling him off. If you raise your voice, this can be construed as further incitement to bark, so is counterproductive. However, by acknowledging the alert he's giving, and making it clear that you have everything under control, this gives a clear signal that there's no need for further barking.

Some dogs bark in order to demand attention, because their owner has reinforced this by giving attention every time they bark. If you simply withdraw, by silently turning away or leaving the room, this soon eliminates this habit. By ignoring demands, but rewarding your dog as soon as he is quiet, you can swiftly retrain him out of displaying pushy habits and he will become much pleasanter company.

## Stay, and wait

These are very useful lessons to teach your dog. Staying still is an essential aspect of good doorbell manners, it can calm him down if he's in an excitable mood, and it can keep him safe if he is about to go too close to a road or is heading towards a dog who doesn't look as if he'll welcome the extra attention.

In dog training parlance, 'stay' means that the dog should remain in position until you go to him, whereas 'wait' means that the dog stays still until you signal him to come to you. The first stage of the instructions are the same for both.

'Dogs bark in order to get our attention – to let us know there's a noise we should be aware of, or a person or another dog passing too close to their territory.'

Duke learns to stay

To teach your dog to 'stay', first ask him to 'sit' and reward him for sitting. Stand directly in front of him, though not so close that you're looming over him, and relax all your muscles. Put your hand out in the 'stop' position and take a step backwards. Don't say anything just yet, as you're simply teaching him to pay attention to your signal at this point. Now take another step back, keeping your hand in the 'stop' position. Say 'Stay', and immediately go to him and reward him with praise and a treat.

Practise this often, when your dog is in a relaxed frame of mind. Each time you practise the 'stay', step further back before returning to him. Only turn your back on him to move away when he's figured out what you're asking of him, otherwise you'd be setting him up for failure and could confuse him. If he seems bored or anxious, stop the training and try again later.

You can use this method to teach your dog to 'wait', but ask him to 'wait' instead of 'stay', and call him over to you for lots of praise and a treat. Remember to increase the distance between you gradually, so that you set him up to succeed every time.

# Leave it

This lesson is invaluable for those times when your dog is about to take something that you don't want him to have, such as food on the counter or table, a resource that belongs to another dog, your kitchen bin if your dog is a bin-raider, and even something unsavoury (to you, but not to him!) encountered during walks. It can also work well for situations where your dog is starting to get overexcited about the presence of another dog. Start the training in-between mealtimes, so that your dog isn't too hungry to be able to pay attention.

Hold a treat in your closed hand, with a portion of it poking out so that your dog can see and smell it. Let him put his nose close to your hand, and wait until he realises that you're not offering the treat and glances away or his nose draws back slightly. As soon as he creates a little distance, give him the treat and lots of praise. Do this several times and then say 'Leave it' as soon as he looks or moves slightly away.

The next step is to have a treat on one open palm and another in a closed hand. Don't let him take the treat from your open palm. As soon as he glances away from the exposed treat, say 'Leave it' and give him the treat in your closed hand.

You can graduate to putting a treat on the floor or a low table, asking him to 'Leave it' and giving him another treat from your hand. The next stage is to put treats or a small bowl of food on the floor and walk him past this on-lead. Reward him with a treat from your hand as soon as he stops focusing on the food you have set out.

After a while you'll find that your dog can be trusted to ignore the snack you left on the coffee table, and to walk away from that fascinating pile of fox scat that he was considering having a good roll in.

'Teaching your dog to lie down can help him to relax.'

## Down

Teaching your dog to lie down can help him to relax, and can also help you to relax during busy times or when you're in the waiting area at your veterinary surgeon's or groomer's.

Hold some treats in your hand and ask your dog to 'sit'. Bring the hand with the treats slowly down to the ground, a few inches in front of his nose. His nose will move downwards to follow the scent, and his body will follow. Slide your hand along the ground a little way so that his body stretches out downwards. As soon as his body touches the floor, say 'Down' and reward him.

Another method you can use is to sit on the floor with your legs bent so that there's a space below your knees. Hold the treat on the far side of your knees as soon as you've gained your dog's attention, so that his body naturally goes into a lying position as he moves through the space to get the treat. Say 'Down' as soon as his belly touches the ground, and reward him.

You can also use a chair or a low table as a space for your dog to move beneath. Once your dog has learned to associate the word 'down' with lying on the ground, you can dispense with any extra aids, but carry on with the praise and rewards.

If you wish to use a hand signal to ask your dog to go 'down', just lower your hand with your palm facing the ground.

## Settle

'Before asking a pacing dog to settle, consider why he is behaving in this way.'

This is a great way to calm down your dog if he's overexcited, restless or anxious. It helps him to relax and can be very useful if your dog tends to hassle guests, beg at the table, or pace the room when he's bored. However, before asking a pacing dog to settle, consider why he is behaving in this way. Is he uncomfortable, or anxious about something? If so, asking him to 'settle' can worsen his distress and you need to find the cause of his discomfort. Does he need to toilet? Is he bored? If he's bored, perhaps he needs more stimulation, so give him extra sniffing time on walks, more company (if possible) or a toy or Kong so that his needs are fulfilled.

There are two methods you can use to teach your dog to settle down. The first one is useful for visits to the vet or groomer and the second one is very effective if your dog is being bothersome through overexcitement.

For the first method, ask your dog to go into the 'down' position. Give him small treats and praise him in a soft, calm tone of voice while you stroke him. Check his paws and ears and run your hand over his ribs, giving treats as you do so. This will accustom him to being checked over at the vet's and shampooed or clipped at the groomer's.

If your dog easily gets excited, the second method works well. Choose an area where you want him to lie down and relax in future. This could be his bed, or a particular corner of the room. Point at the area, say 'Settle' in a calm, firm tone of voice, and throw a treat onto that area. He will go over to collect his reward. As soon as he's eaten his reward, ask him to lie 'down' as you throw another treat onto that area. If he starts to get up, use the 'stop' signal and point again at the area you want him to lie in, rewarding him immediately when he cooperates. He will soon respond when you simply point and say 'Settle'.

## Doorbell manners and greeting guests

A dog who greets guests by flinging himself at them in a frenzy of excitement, knocking them off-balance, leaving fur on their clothes or even shredding or snagging them, is guaranteed to reduce the number of visitors you have – especially those who are already nervous of dogs. Some 'doggy' people don't mind being mugged by a four-legged bundle of enthusiasm, and may even encourage your dog to jump up or leap about, but many people find this behaviour unnerving and intimidating. Teaching good guest-greeting skills are a 'must' for dog owners.

Your dog will need to have learned to 'sit' or lie 'down' before you help him graduate in greeting guests politely. You'll need the assistance of a patient friend for practice while he learns what's expected of him each time the doorbell rings or there's a knock on your door.

First, think about what usually happens when your doorbell rings. You drop whatever you're doing and move swiftly towards the door. Your dog senses that something exciting is happening, so he gets keyed up. It becomes a struggle for supremacy of position as you both jostle to get to the door first. You may get impatient or annoyed, especially if your dog is in the way. Your dog then further senses your highly charged emotional state and becomes even more wound up. You open the door feeling flustered (and possibly stressed) and your guest is faced with a hyperactive bouncing bundle of fur who isn't sure whether he should be protecting his owner from an intruder or whether it's 'fun time' and he'll be treated to lots of extra attention.

To teach doorbell manners, set a time for a friend to come and help out, on a day when your friend has at least two hours to spare. If it's pouring with rain on the pre-arranged day, reschedule because your friend will most likely be on the wrong side of the door for some time! Some dogs learn doorbell manners very quickly, while others may need repeated training over several hours, so gather

'Teaching good guest-greeting skills are a "must" for dog owners.'

your patience and plenty of high-quality treats. If your dog isn't food oriented, choose at least two favourite toys that you only use as rewards for desired behaviour.

Ask your friend to ring the doorbell or knock on the door at the prearranged time. Even if your dog rushes towards the door, make sure you walk calmly and slowly so that no extra excitement is generated. Stop several feet from the door and call your dog. Use one of the chosen rewards as a lure if he ignores you. Ask him to sit, and praise and reward him as soon as he complies. Keep him in the 'sit' position and move to open the door. If he gets up, place him back in the 'sit' position and reward him. If you're using toys, you can exchange one for the other. Stay calm! Keep this up until you can actually touch the door handle.

When he's sitting, start to open the door. If he gets up, immediately shut the door and start over. You'll need to do this every time he rises, until he stays calm while you let your friend in. If he then becomes excited, ask your friend to immediately step outside, and start over.

Your dog will soon learn that he's unable to follow through on what was previously the rewarding behaviour of getting to the door first and bouncing around your friend. There's now a fulsome reward for sitting calmly, so, with consistent training, this is the behaviour he will follow through on in future.

'The easiest way to teach your dog to leave you in peace while you eat is to make a rule that no one ever gives him a morsel of food from their plate.'

## Table manners

The easiest way to teach your dog to leave you in peace while you eat is to make a rule that no one ever gives him a morsel of food from their plate. However, if your dog has learned that sitting close to you and begging, nudging, whining or drooling brings the reward of some of your food, you'll need to start over with teaching him good mealtime manners.

Dogs are opportunist eaters – they're naturally hard-wired to snaffle up unattended food. Some dogs, especially rescue dogs who have gone hungry in the past, will see any food as theirs for the taking – and who can blame them, when they think that every meal may be their last? They may counter surf to help themselves if you leave food in the open, or they may stand over you and hassle you or look hungry while you're eating. Even dogs who have previously experienced near-starvation soon learn that this isn't acceptable, if you're calm, firm and consistent about the house rules regarding food.

If your dog is a counter surfer, you can nip this in the bud by never leaving unattended food where it's accessible, and by not allowing them access to the kitchen counters while you're preparing food. As your dog goes to jump up, swiftly and calmly step sideways so that your body blocks access. You can say 'Off' if you want to, but it's best to stay silent and simply put yourself in the way. If you prefer to say 'Off', remember to praise him as soon as his paws touch the floor, so that he understands what you expect from him. Avoid looking at him while you do this, because that could be construed as rewarding attention or even a confrontation. As soon as your dog has all four paws on the ground, praise him and carry on with preparing your meal. Most dogs, even the very persistent ones, learn to stop counter surfing within three days when this method is used.

Dogs who beg while you're eating are a nuisance, and being harassed or drooled over by a determined dog isn't conducive to good digestion. The first step towards remedying this is to make a rule to never again feed your dog from your plate – this removes the dog's reward for his behaviour, and dogs soon stop carrying on with habits that don't bring any pay-off. You can use the 'settle' method to encourage your dog to go to his bed or give you space while you're eating. If you're having a snack on the sofa and your dog wants a portion, again you can send him to his bed. Some dogs are very persistent at first, so shielding your plate or turning away will give the message that he won't be getting anything while you're eating. By blocking his access and sending him away, you are showing him that his attention isn't welcome at this time.

If you allow your dog to eat some of your leftovers, take these to his bowl after you have finished eating, and ask him to 'sit' while you put in the scraps. Some foods are very bad for dogs' health, so avoid letting him have anything that contains chocolate, grapes, raisins, sultanas, coffee, tea, yeast dough, onions, mushrooms, garlic, spices, avocados, salt, alcohol or cooked bones.

'A tight lead that's attached to the collar can cause serious health problems for your dog.'

# Loose leash walking

One of the most common reasons why a behaviourist is called in is that the owners have come to dread walk time. Being dragged along behind your dog, grimly holding on to the lead as he charges exuberantly ahead, is no fun. A tight lead that's attached to the collar can cause serious health problems for your dog; damage to his tender throat area, convulsions and blindness can result in dogs who suddenly leap forward or whose owners jerk hard on the lead. The trainers who subscribe to dominance methods tell us dogs pull on the leash because they wants to be 'alphas' and lead the hunt. This isn't what's in your dog's mind at all!

Loose leash walking

Consider a walk from your dog's perspective. He may have been indoors for hours, with nothing to do except rest while you were busy or out at work. When the lead comes out he feels a surge of excitement. He may run around and head for the door, to make sure you don't leave him behind. Once you're outside he'll want to absorb all the scents that have appeared since his last walk, because these give him an update on the latest news. He'll be deluged with a plethora of fascinating stimuli and will want to take it all in. Sniffing around also gives him much-needed mental stimulation, which is as important to his wellbeing as the physical exercise gained from the walk. It's no wonder that he gets excited and forges ahead with gusto!

If your dog is pulling on the lead in his eagerness to use up some energy and gather as much information as possible, the tension created by a tight lead will only prompt him to pull harder in order to escape it. The trick to loose leash walking is to make sure the lead never gets taut.

A harness is much more comfortable for dogs than a collar and lead (though your dog should still wear a collar with a tag containing your contact details). The easiest type for you to put on, and the most comfy for your dog, is a Perfect Fit harness that clips closed at the sides and is well padded to ensure that no areas chafe or rub. You can find these at www.dog-games-shop.co.uk. See the help list for contact details. A good harness gives you more control over your dog and it makes walks much more pleasant for both of you. A long lead is better than a short one, because you're less likely to pull on it and you can also give him more leeway to sniff around.

If your dog pulls on his lead, he'll most likely display marked signs of excitement when you prepare to take him out, so your first step in training him is to calm him down before you leave your home. If he jumps around at the sight of his leash, put his lead away and go and sit down for a minute. Repeat this until he's calm, then step calmly in front of him while you open the door. This helps to prevent the surge of adrenalin that occurs when he sees freedom beckoning, and starts off the walk on the best foot (and paw).

## Tried and tested methods

There are three methods you can use when your dog pulls while out. The first method involves stopping and standing still as soon as the lead goes taut. Your dog will naturally stop too, and look around to see why you're not moving forward. As soon as he stops, praise and reward him and then slowly move forward. Keep repeating this until he gets the message that the walk won't proceed unless he stays with you. With particularly excitable dogs you can use the second method of swiftly changing direction each time he pulls, so that he's following you instead of dragging you behind him. Remember to keep the lead as loose as possible.

The third method reduces the likelihood that you'll have to keep stopping and starting or changing direction. It works very well with dogs who are very food or toy oriented. Have a pocketful of treats or a couple of his favourite toys with you when you go for a walk. A squeaky toy or ball is best, because squeezing it immediately gets his attention. Hold the lead loosely in one hand and keep your free hand, holding the rewards, by your thigh and within scent distance of your dog's nose. He'll stay close to you because he'll want the reward of the treats or toys. Each time he moves close to you, praise and reward him. He'll soon learn that it's far more exciting to stay near you than to forge ahead.

## Home grooming

All dogs, even those with short coats, need regular brushing. This helps to remove dead hair, dust and dirt, and it gives you an opportunity to check that your dog has no sore areas or lumps and bumps. If your dog has a long coat, you'll need to groom him at least once daily with a brush that's appropriate for his coat-type, so that he doesn't get uncomfortable knots and tangles in his fur. If he has a short, smooth coat, once or twice weekly with a soft brush will do.

'All dogs, even those with short coats, need regular brushing.'

Some dogs enjoy being groomed and are actively cooperative. Others dislike having certain areas touched, especially if they have tangled fur or painful health issues such as arthritis. You can make grooming time pleasant for both of you by creating a positive association with his hairbrush.

Only use the brush during grooming sessions. If you tease him with it or use it as a tug toy, your dog will be very reluctant to stay still while you brush him. Call your dog to you and ask him to sit or lie down. Gently smooth your hand, followed by the brush, along his side (the least threatening area for your dog). As you do this, praise him and give him a treat. If he is clearly anxious, end the session and start afresh a few hours later. With very anxious dogs you can simply show him the brush and give him a treat, then put the brush away. Before long he'll be wagging his tail when he sees you get the brush out. As he gets used to the feeling of the brush, and is more focused on you and the rewards, gradually extend the brushing range to other areas.

# Summing Up

- Keep training sessions short so that your dog doesn't lose interest.

- Break down lessons into small increments and proceed at a pace that is comfortable for your dog.

- Practise training at home first, where there are less distractions.

- Teach your dog to have a positive association with his name.

- Good timing is vital during toilet training.

- One of the most important things to teach your dog is to stop when asked.

- Dogs understand our tones of voice and body language, so use both during training.

- Make training sessions fun.

- Ignore unwanted behaviour and reward the behaviour you wish to encourage.

- If your dog seems bored or anxious, stop the training session and try again later.

- Avoid letting your dog run free beyond the garden until he has learned good recall skills.

- Teaching your dog to 'settle' helps to calm him down if he's overexcited.

- Loose-lead walking makes walks a pleasure instead of a challenge.

- Looking at your dog's reactions from his perspective helps you to understand his behaviour.

# Chapter Three

## Social Training

Dogs are social creatures and over millennia we have capitalised on this in order to gain the most from their skills in herding, pulling heavy loads, sniffing, hunting and guarding. Selective breeding has resulted in our modern dogs who need company to the extent that they are anxious and unhappy when left alone for long periods. Studies have revealed that, when given the choice between canine company and human company, most dogs will choose to be with humans. The inter-species bond which has developed over time is truly remarkable.

Although it may seem, from this, that most dogs are born with innate social skills, these need to be deliberately developed. Some skills, such as the ability to decipher and display certain body language signals, are instinctive, but their development is dependent upon good mothering during the early weeks and good training from the people they live with whilst they grow from puppies, to adolescents, to mature adults.

It can help to look at this from a human perspective. Human babies are hard-wired to focus on human faces and to desire and respond to social interaction – their survival depends upon how well cared for they are while they are too small and helpless to fend for themselves. Yet they need to be taught appropriate ways of behaving and of treating others, otherwise they would grow up to be socially inept and would be at risk of alienating others to the point of becoming social outcasts.

It's no different with dogs. During the first few weeks the rough and tumble with their littermates helps to teach them about body language. They learn to deal with frustration if another littermate beats them to the feeding post. They learn to squeal and walk away if a playful nip hurts them; and they learn that their mother will respond to irritating behaviour by grumbling at them or absenting herself. During this time, if they are fortunate enough to be handled gently and

'Studies have revealed that, when given the choice between canine company and human company, most dogs will choose to be with humans.'

regularly, they also learn that humans are friendly creatures whose attentions become welcomed and even sought for. Puppies who started life in the horrors that are puppy mills/farms have little or no opportunity for social interaction and often have problems relating to humans and other dogs as they grow up.

There are specific windows of opportunity for learning. If these crucial times pass by without a puppy receiving the experiences he needs in order to learn good social skills, this lack can damage him emotionally and socially for the rest of his life, resulting in fear and aggression towards humans and other dogs. It's vitally important to socialise puppies, especially with people, during the critical period of four to twelve weeks of age. Doing this has a long-term positive impact on dogs' personalities and behaviour.

The earlier social training begins, the better, but dogs are never too old to learn new skills if they are taught compassionately and with respect for their feelings. You will discover more about canine communication and how to 'read' your dog in the next chapter, and this will help you both to enjoy all aspects of training.

'The earlier social training begins, the better.'

In the previous chapter you discovered how to teach your dog good doorbell manners, but interactions with people occur frequently, both indoors and out, so you'll want your dog to be polite, wherever you are with him. You'll also want your dog to accept the presence of other dogs in the vicinity when he's out with you. The most common complaints about unruly dogs are concerned with jumping up, pawing, barking at strangers, and fear-based issues such as nervousness and fear-aggression.

## Child safety

Dogs and children can make wonderful companions for each other, but an important factor in training your dog is keeping children safe around him, and keeping him safe around children. Never leave a dog and child together unattended! The horrific accounts of badly or mortally injured children that have occasionally been reported in the news mostly occurred when there was inadequate supervision.

Ask any children in your environment not to tease or engage in rough play with your dog. Tugging games can lead to tears or injuries if sharp canine teeth catch flesh instead of the tug-toy. Ensure that your dog has a quiet place to retreat to if he's had enough of children's company, and make it a rule that no one disturbs him when he's in his 'safe space'.

Petting should only be engaged in when you are present to interpret your dog's body language. Some young children can get carried away and pat too hard, which makes rather sensitive dogs anxious or fearful, and children rarely understand 'Please back off' signals until the dog feels driven to growl or snap.

When you introduce an unknown child to your dog, ask him or her to give your dog space instead of crowding close to him. Tell the child to make slow movements and keep his or her voice soft so as not to scare your dog. The high-pitched voices and squeals of children can frighten some dogs and set off the prey drive in others. If the child stands still, your dog will most likely move forward for a polite sniff when he's ready to make friends. Watch your dog's body language. When he seems comfortable you can let the child stroke his side, avoiding his face and the top of his head. Hugs restrict your dog's ability to escape if he's anxious, so make sure that the child is considerate of your dog. Remind the child to treat your dog gently and with respect.

The bond between a child and their beloved dog can be very special, and many adults fondly recall the dog friends of their early years. Dogs know just how to offer comfort and company to a sad or lonely child. They always keep the secrets that are whispered in their ears. They can be wonderful playmates and partners in mischief and they are unstinting in their devotion.

# Jumping up at people

Dogs learned as tiny puppies that if they jumped up and licked their mother's face, she would disgorge food for them. They also jumped at each other as part of their rough and tumble games with littermates. If your dog jumps up to paw at or lick you, this doesn't mean that he's anticipating food (though he may leap up to see what you're putting in his bowl if it's dinner time and he hasn't learned the table manners described in chapter 2). Jumping up at you when you return home after an absence usually means that your dog is happy and excited to see you. A small dog may not cause much damage, other than a few scratches, or some snags in your clothing, but a large dog could knock you flying – and can be an intimidating prospect for people who aren't sure of his intentions.

Your dog will repeat behaviour that has previously resulted in a reward for him, and any attention given to your dog when he jumps up at you will be construed as a reward. This includes telling him off, or even trying to push him away – it becomes a game, in his view. The solution lies in removing the reward of your attention. If you silently turn your back on your dog and cross your arms over your chest, he'll most likely be nonplussed at first and may try approaching you from another angle. If he does this, simply turn away again. Avoid speaking to him or looking at him while he's jumping. As soon as he calms down and all four paws are on the ground, praise him, ask him to 'sit' and give him a treat.

Jumping up at strangers, especially out of doors, can be your dog's way of saying 'Back off and give me (and my owner) more space.'

'Remember to always praise your dog for staying calm, so that you continue to reinforce his training.'

When you have visitors, or friends stop for a chat while you're out with your dog, ask them to follow the same procedure given above. It can help to brief guests in advance about what you're teaching your dog, and why, before they arrive, so that they know what to do if your dog jumps at them.

Dogs quickly learn to greet people politely when you use this method. Remember to always praise your dog for staying calm, so that you continue to reinforce his training.

## Jumping at other dogs

Puppies leap and clamber all over each other, and when they move to their forever home they initially view all other dogs as playmates and act towards them in the same way as they did with their littermates. Some adult dogs are very tolerant and will put up with being clambered over, but others take umbrage at the rude pup who is disturbing their peace. Most puppies soon learn that a growl from another dog is a signal to back off, but it's your responsibility to teach your puppy to behave well around other dogs. It isn't fair on an adult dog if he growls while being pestered, and is then told off for it – and chastising a dog for grumbling may mean that he then stops giving a warning and goes straight to the biting stage. And it wouldn't be fair on your puppy if you allowed him to continue to irritate another dog and he suffered the consequences. A baby gate can come in useful if you have a puppy and an older dog, as you can separate the dogs when necessary, without either dog feeling excluded or banished.

Make sure your puppy has plenty of opportunities for socialising, on lead at first with other dogs, so that it doesn't become a big deal if he does see a dog in the vicinity. Habituation will reduce your puppy's level of interest. If he charges towards another dog and that dog looks anxious or tense, immediately call him to you in a happy, excited voice so that he runs to see what you have for him. As soon as he returns to you, reward him handsomely. If you do this consistently, he'll become calmer in the presence of other dogs as well as getting good practice at recall.

Adult dogs who had few opportunities for socialising when younger can become overexcited and jump all over other dogs when they first meet them. If your dog does this, first work on his loose-leash training and then take him out on his lead to places where other dogs are walked. In chapter 5 you will find out how to get your dog's attention by using the 'watch me' training, so if you wish to skip ahead and read this before going out with your boisterous adult, this may come in very useful. Keep your dog's focus on you and use high-quality rewards that will take his mind off the other dogs. If he still becomes overexcited, calmly turn and walk in the opposite direction, away from the other dogs.

Walks with friends who have calm, well-behaved dogs can make a real impact on your dog's socialising skills. Dogs learn from each other, so if your dog has the opportunity to be around other dogs who aren't easily ruffled, he will be more inclined to behave as they do. Remember, though, that it is your responsibility to immediately step in if your dog is being a nuisance.

**'It's your responsibility to teach your puppy to behave well around other dogs.'**

## Pawing

Pawing is a way of demanding your attention. It's similar to a young child tugging at your arm or clothing and it can be annoying if you're busy or are trying to concentrate. Pawing is a learned behaviour. If your dog does this, it's because, in the past, you have given him the attention he's seeking – you may even have thought it was cute.

You can teach your dog to stop being so demanding by simply withholding attention each time he does this. Turn away, or leave the room, for a few moments. When your dog is relaxed, praise him. This will teach him that there's no point in pawing at you because the desired effect isn't forthcoming – but calm, undemanding behaviour brings the reward he hoped for.

## Barking at strangers and strange dogs

If your dog does this, the most likely reason is that he's feeling rather anxious or scared, so he barks to tell the person or dog not to approach too closely. If a strange person intrudes into what you consider to be your safe personal space, by standing too close or touching you, you may step back. If you feel confident enough, you may even ask the person to back off. Barking is your dog's way of saying this too, and you'll know if he's feeling anxious because he's likely to move backwards while he's barking.

'Keep your dog's focus on you and use high-quality rewards that will take his mind off the other dogs.'

The solution is to teach your dog that you're willing to protect him from perceived intrusion or potential harm. You can do this by creating more distance between your dog and the object of anxiety, by moving away or even turning and walking off in the opposite direction.

Once your dog becomes aware that you're in charge and can take action to ease his worries, he'll start to feel more confident. The next step is to help him to deal with situations that cause him anxiety.

First, observe how much space your dog needs around him in order to feel safe and comfortable. Some dogs need several metres of personal space, while others only react anxiously if an 'intruder' comes within touching distance. Take your time in teaching him to cope with infringements on his 'safe area'. If you try to rush him into coping, this will only increase his stress levels. Your aim will be to gradually increase his tolerance in such a way that he eventually starts to associate the proximity of strangers as a source of pleasure and reward.

Next, take him just two or three inches closer than he can usually tolerate before barking. While you do this, distract him with treats or toys and by talking calmly and softly to him. The aim of this is to make sure your dog doesn't notice that he's slightly out of his proximity comfort zone. After a minute, move away with him and keep praising him. If he notices and starts barking, calmly walk him away and try again another day.

This can be a slow process with some very anxious dogs, but even with very reactive dogs it usually works within a few weeks, if you persevere and take the training at a pace that is comfortable for your dog.

# Timid dogs

A number of reasons can cause dogs to be timid. A nervous mother who distrusts people transfers this to her puppies during their infancy and this has lifelong repercussions on their personalities. Lack of socialisation can make dogs fearful of new people or dogs. Unpleasant experiences at any time of life, such as mistreatment from a human or aggression from another dog, can have such a traumatic effect that the dog shies away from contact.

There's a big difference in outlook between timid dogs and naturally quiet, introverted dogs. Introverted dogs prefer a calm, quiet environment and company, but enjoy interaction with others on their own terms. Timid dogs are fearful and tend to be highly strung, reacting anxiously to anything and anyone unknown in case this poses a threat to them.

A timid dog may step back when approached, or take shelter behind his owner. He may display the classic signs of anxiety – trembling, lowering his body to make himself appear smaller, tucking his tail between his legs, pinning back his ears, rolling onto his back, or even wetting himself. If your dog acts like this when meeting new people or situations, avoid any temptation to force him to engage. This will only increase his fear, and he may even feel so threatened that he growls, snarls or nips in his desperation to create distance between himself and the source of anxiety.

## Give them time

Timid dogs need to be given space and plenty of time. You'll need a lot of patience while you gently teach him, without using any coercion, that it's safe for him to step out of his protective shell. Following him around, trying to get his attention, will only cause him to become more fearful. Imagine if you were

'Once your dog becomes aware that you're in charge and can take action to ease his worries, he'll start to feel more confident.'

scared of, say, clowns (a common fear in humans, apparently!), and one kept chasing around after you, trying to get close. Thinking of how you would feel in that situation can give insight into the effect that human attention-seeking would have on your timid dog.

Let the dog come to you. Just sit or stand quietly, without looking at the dog. Position your body so that you're facing sideways, away from the dog, so that you seem smaller and less threatening. Speak very softly, and scatter tasty treats around the area, from further away right through to close to you. Wait. After a while he will be curious enough to cautiously approach. Use your peripheral vision instead of looking directly at him and continue to speak very quietly and reassuringly. Eventually, in his own time, he will come to you. Some dogs who have experienced abuse in the past may take days to come close enough to make physical contact with you, while others may be reassured enough by your non-threatening body language to come over in just a few minutes. When this does happen, take care not to reach out and touch him. If he nuzzles you or sniffs you, you can very slowly and gently let your hand brush his side, avoiding the top of his head. Eventually he will learn that you can be trusted not to harm him.

'Timid dogs need to be given space and plenty of time.'

A timid dog needs your protection if other people are determined to make friends with him. Explain that he needs space while he figures out whether he wants to be approached or be stroked, and ask them to respect this. Unfortunately, often people who like dogs can assume that every dog will welcome their attention, so you may have to step between them and your dog if they persist in trying to pet him. Be assertive without being confrontational – your dog needs you to be his champion.

Timid dogs can blossom into friendly dogs if they are treated considerately and with patience. It can be immensely rewarding when a previously scared, nervous dog learns that people can be trusted. When he offers the gift of devotion and affection, the relationship can seem even more special than with a dog who views everyone as his best friend.

# Fear-based issues

Most behaviour issues in dogs have their roots in fear or anxiety. Timidity and nervousness, as explained in the previous section, is a fear-based issue. So, usually, is aggression, which is a very misunderstood issue in dog behaviour.

Unless a dog has been trained to be aggressive, as with guard dogs or (sadly, this still occurs illegally) fighting dogs, the majority of aggression issues are caused by fear. Dogs (and most other animals, including humans) take whichever of three courses of action that seem wisest to them when they feel threatened. These are the three Fs: freeze, flight and fight. If a dog feels that he can stand still and avoid conflict, or run away from it, he will usually choose not to fight – this is the last recourse, because injuries could reduce his chances of survival. However, when a dog is on-lead, the freeze option is possible, but the flight option isn't, so he's more likely to react to unwelcome attention by giving a warning growl and lunging.

One main cause of fear-aggression is lack of socialisation during puppyhood. If a dog learns to mix well with other dogs, fights due to fear of them are far less likely to occur. This is one of the reasons why socialising your dog through puppy classes, visiting friends with dogs, and group walks are so valuable. Another common cause of this type of aggression is fear of other dogs (or dogs of specific sizes or colours) after being badly frightened by an attack or very rough play in the past.

If your dog has actually attacked other dogs, your best course of action is to enlist the help of a qualified behaviourist or trainer who uses only positive methods. However, if his problem is growling, barking or lunging you can work on his training by enlisting the help of a friend who has a calm, well-socialised dog.

Choose a large area, such as a field or park, and go there at a time when it's unlikely to be busy. Take plenty of rewards with you and keep both dogs on-lead. Ask your friend to take his or her dog to the far end of the area so that there is a good distance between you and them. Keep the dogs on your far sides, so that you and your friend are on the inside. Walk your dog parallel to the dog in the distance, going in the same direction. Reward him as you walk along, so that his focus is more on you than the other side of the walking area. If your dog reacts, swiftly turn and walk in the opposite direction, cheerfully

'Most behaviour issues in dogs have their roots in fear or anxiety.'

saying a short phrase such as 'Let's go!' as you turn. As soon as he is calm, reward him with praise and a treat, then turn around so that you're again walking parallel to your friend and dog. Repeat this each time he reacts and be patient with him if he doesn't seem to be learning as well as you hoped.

When your dog is comfortably walking parallel at a distance, you can close that distance just a little, keeping the dogs on the outside. Take it slowly, so that your dog doesn't become anxious or overwhelmed. As your dog grows more used to the presence of the other dog, and stops reacting, you can gradually close the distance more, and shift position so that the dogs are on the inside, walking parallel to each other. Avoid any temptation to stop and introduce them, even if your dog seems calm.

'It can take time, patience, compassion and persistence to help a dog through his fears.'

When your dog has stayed calm for a while, and he shows by his relaxed body posture and a wagging tail that he's interested in an introduction, ask your friend to move forward so that you are following him or her. Your dog will be able to catch the interesting rear-end scents of your friend's dog, and won't be put in the scary position of a face-to-face confrontation. If all seems well, gradually catch up so that he can sniff the other dog and make friends. If you notice any signs of tension, immediately walk away with him and start over again with the training. However, if all is going well, you could then progress to letting them play off-lead together in a safe enclosed space.

It can take time, patience, compassion and persistence to help a dog through his fears, but if your dog feels safe with you, and understands that you will keep him out of danger, he will learn to relax around other dogs.

# Summing Up

- Dogs are social animals.

- Early social skills are learned with the mother and littermates.

- If a dog hasn't received positive social experiences during the first weeks, this can affect his later development.

- The windows of opportunity for learning social skills are between four to twelve weeks of age.

- Dogs are never too old to learn new skills.

- Any attention you give to your dog when he jumps up will reinforce his behaviour.

- It is your responsibility to teach your dog to be polite with other dogs.

- Giving your dog plenty of positive opportunities for socialising will increase his skills.

- Many behaviour issues are based on anxiety and fear.

- Teaching your dog that he is safe with you will increase his confidence.

# Chapter Four

# Effective Two-Way Communication

Unless we've made an effort to understand body language, we humans tend to mostly subconsciously pick up the messages that other people around us are silently transmitting. Dogs spend far less time vocalising than we do, and they pay very close attention to the body language of other dogs and of people. Understanding and acting on these subtle messages is how they keep themselves safe.

Your dog can pick up on your frame of mind and emotional state without you needing to say a word. If you're feeling happy, your dog will most likely act playful. If you're sad, he may rest close by you, or put his head in your lap to offer his support and give you comfort. If you're angry he will steer clear of you, or will display his own silent signals that proclaim his anxiety and his eagerness to prove that he's trying to calm you down. How does he know how you are feeling? He can read you like an open book!

A great deal of confusion arises because we misinterpret what a dog is really saying. The way he's wagging his tail may seem friendly, so it's a shock if he then growls a warning when you approach him. That display of teeth may look scary, until you discover that your dog is doing his version of a smile of pleasure or ingratiation.

Dogs have evolved alongside us over many thousands of years. Their survival depends upon their ability to know whether the human close by is a friend or foe. Yet it's only fairly recently that scientists have studied the silent language of dogs and discovered how extraordinarily sophisticated this is. Learning to 'speak dog' can have a profound effect on our relationships with our dogs.

'Your dog can pick up on your frame of mind and emotional state without you needing to say a word.'

# Learning the body language

The following sections describe dog body language that relates to different mental and emotional states. When you have read these, perhaps you'll observe your dog more closely and understand exactly what he's trying to communicate to you! Following these sections is information on how you can deliberately use your body language in order to communicate effectively with your dog.

## Happiness

It's always a delight to witness a dog who's feeling happy. His bright eyes, wagging tail and upright posture speak volumes. He may open his mouth, revealing his teeth in the canine version of a smile. He has a light step and bouncing walk, and he may dance around or play bow. His ears and facial muscles are relaxed.

'Learning to "speak dog" can have a profound effect on our relationships with our dogs.'

## Playfulness

Dogs invite each other (and humans) to play by performing a 'play bow'. The front of the body is lowered, with the front legs extended, as the rear end goes up in the air. You may also see your dog play bowing at another dog if he feels anxious about the dog's motives towards him – this is a way of signalling that he's no threat, he's not interested in conflict and would rather be friends.

## Fear, anxiety or worry

If your dog is frightened, anxious, worried or concerned, he will stay still and lower his body and head to make himself appear smaller. He'll turn his head away, and may yawn or lick his lips and nose. A scared dog will shift his weight backwards onto his hind legs, cringe, tuck his tail between his legs and may try to hide behind you or shrink away. He may display what is termed a 'submissive grin' to signal conciliation. You'll find out more about the silent language of a stressed or anxious dog in the section on page 54 on calming signals. His ears will go back and, if you look closely, there will be little wrinkles of tension on his face, especially around the eye area. If he is anxious he may sit or lie down, to show that he's no threat.

An anxious, uneasy or uncomfortable dog will also use redirection tactics to show that he's not interested in any form of confrontation. He may turn away and sniff or scratch at the ground, or clean his genitals, or sit and scratch himself.

## Sadness

Dogs do experience sadness, depression and grief. This shows as a loss of appetite and energy, a disinterest in interaction and play, and dull, unfocused eyes. His body language is similar to that of an anxious dog. His ears, tail and body will be low, and he'll avoid looking at you. He may choose to separate himself by staying on his bed or going to a quiet area.

## Anger

If your dog is gearing up for a confrontation he'll stand as tall as possible, with his tail held high, to make sure he looks more intimidating. His body will be tense, and the hackles will rise on his shoulders and back, to make him appear even larger. He'll shift the front of his body forward, so that his weight rests over his shoulders and front legs. His eyes will protrude and grow round, and it's likely that you will see the sclera (the whites of his eyes) which aren't usually visible in dogs. His ears will go back so that they're close to the sides of his head and the muscles on his face will tense. He may growl or curl back his lips to show his teeth. An angry dog may wag his tail slowly from side to side.

## Jealousy

Some dogs can get jealous over attention or resources, and this can be directed towards other dogs or towards humans. It's a common issue in dogs who have lived alone with their owner and received a great deal of attention and affection, who then feel usurped by an intruder if their owner gets involved in a romantic relationship.

'Dogs do experience sadness, depression and grief.'

This may be displayed by the dog pushing himself in-between the owner and other dog or person, jumping up, attention-seeking by barking, chewing or carrying out misdemeanours that are out of character for him, and even through displaying the signals of anger in the previous section.

## Stress/calming signals

Dogs use a number of signals to communicate that they are taking steps to calm themselves when they feel stressed. These are used partly for the dog's own comfort, and to indicate to you, or another dog, that they intend no harm.

Norwegian dog trainer Turid Rugaas calls these 'calming signals', and has written an excellent book called *On Talking Terms with Dogs: Calming Signals*, which describes in detail how you can recognise and respond to fourteen of these.

'Dogs use a number of signals to communicate that they are taking steps to calm themselves when they feel stressed.'

Calming signals include averting the head or eyes, turning away bodily, standing or lying very still, moving slowly (especially in a curving motion), sitting or lying down, licking the nose, yawning, play bowing, wagging the tail gently, moving away to casually sniff at the ground, and 'splitting up' – moving in-between two dogs or people who are squaring up for an argument.

Some of these signals are part of the dog's repertoire of polite canine manners. In particular, dogs naturally avoid looking each other in the eye because this is usually a prelude to conflict. It is remarkable that a dog who has learned to trust us will deliberately allow eye contact, and even seek it, with us, because this goes against the grain of good manners with their own species.

If you notice your dog displaying stress/calming signals, you can either remove him from the source of anxiety or give him space so that he can relax. Think about what could be making him feel uncomfortable. Perhaps a stranger has moved too close to him, or he senses that you're not in the best of moods. Maybe another dog is being too boisterous or pushy, or something is going on around him that is making him feel anxious.

# Does your dog feel guilt?

It's commonly believed that when you come home to find your dog has done something undesirable (pooped indoors, perhaps, or chewed the furniture) he cringes and looks sorry because he feels guilty. This isn't the case. Psychologist Alexandra Horowitz conducted a study into whether or not dogs feel guilt. The research showed that the dogs couldn't associate their owners' annoyance or anger with something they had done earlier – their displays of cringing, looking away, hiding and looking embarrassed were sparked by feelings of anxiety or fear over their owners' clear signals of disapproval. The dogs were simply (and eloquently) responding to the emotions of their owners.

If your dog has done something 'wrong' (bearing in mind that this is probably only wrong in your eyes, and may be considered normal, acceptable behaviour by him!) and he senses your disapproval, he will try to appease you. As well as using the signals in the previous paragraph, this may take the form of tucking in his tail, blinking, yawning, lip-licking, licking you in an ingratiating manner and using all the calming signals in his repertoire that he feels may help defuse the situation.

# Communicating with your dog through body language

Because of their long association with humans, dogs are experts at reading our body language, and will pay closer attention to this than to our words. Much of our body language is unconscious, and it can be useful to observe how you carry yourself when you're feeling different emotions. If you are tense, anxious or afraid, your body tightens up, your shoulders become hunched, and you may clench your teeth or hands. When you're relaxed, your body is loose and fluid and your eyes are softer. It's harder to deceive your dog than it is to fool other people around you, because your dog will notice even micro-movements in your muscles that most humans are unaware of.

A classic example is when you're thinking of taking your dog for a walk. You may wonder whether your dog is telepathic, because as soon as you think about going out, he'll be up and ready to come with you. This is because he observes you closely, and registers all your unconscious habits that are easily visible through your body language. Perhaps you take a deep breath, sigh, sit up straight, or stretch your back. Perhaps you glance towards him, or towards your phone, keys, or the area where you keep his lead. Your dog will immediately know what's running through your mind!

You can deliberately use your body language to convey a message to your dog. It's also very useful with strange dogs who are unsure about your motives.

## I'm no threat to you

'You can deliberately use your body language to convey a message to your dog.'

Avoid eye contact and use your peripheral vision instead of looking directly at a dog, to tell him that you have no intention of harming or challenging him. Stand slightly sideways instead of head-on, as this makes you seem smaller and less threatening. Keep your body, face and hands relaxed, and make sure your eyes aren't open wide. You can even blink slowly, to help calm the dog. Move slowly and keep your voice soft and low. Avoid standing over the dog or touching the vulnerable areas of his head and the back of his neck.

## I disapprove of this behaviour

Usually just a 'look' will make this clear to your dog. Dogs are very sensitive to the ways in which we look at them. When you're feeling affectionate your eyes will be soft and your face relaxed. When you're irritated or disapproving, you are likely to give him a short hard glance, with narrowed eyes. He'll immediately know how you're feeling.

Turning your body away from him and crossing your arms signals that you're not threatening him but you are also not willing to interact with him.

## I'm very happy with you

You'll instinctively display your pleasure when you feel affectionate by softening your eyes, smiling and using a certain tone of voice. Your movements are lighter, and you may reach out to stroke, pat or ruffle your dog's fur. Your body lowers, especially the upper body, and you'll seek eye contact with him.

It can be fascinating to observe how your dog reacts to your body language, and to watch how he responds when you 'read' him correctly. This two-way non-verbal communication strengthens the bond between you and dog and enhances your relationship.

'It can be fascinating to observe how your dog reacts to your body language, and to watch how he responds when you "read" him correctly.'

# Summing Up

▨ Dogs pay very close attention to our body language.

▨ We need to closely observe dogs' silent signals in order to interpret their feelings and intentions.

▨ The body language of dogs is extraordinarily sophisticated.

▨ Observing how your dog carries himself, and whether his muscles are tense or relaxed, gives you instant access to his state of mind and intentions.

▨ Dogs experience emotions that we recognise as happiness, anxiety, fear, anger, jealousy, sadness and grief.

▨ Dogs use redirection tactics and calming signals to help themselves cope with stress and to show people and other dogs that they intend no harm.

▨ You can consciously use body language in order to communicate effectively with your dog.

▨ When you understand your dog's body language, and use clear signals in your body language, this strengthens the bond between you.

# Chapter Five

# How To Get Your Dog's Attention

Every aspect of training your dog involves gaining and keeping his attention while you teach him how to figure out what you want from him and how he can achieve this. He'll understand how you're feeling by the body language you're displaying, even in the early days of your relationship, but it may take him a while to get used to your gestures, tones of voice and certain words. If you have adopted a rescue dog who has had unpleasant experiences in the past, you will need to tone down extravagant gestures, such as flinging your arms wide open to invite him to run towards you, in case these make him anxious. If you have a puppy or young dog, he may respond faster to large gestures because he finds these stimulating and exciting.

When we wish to gain the attention of another person, we will touch them or speak to them. However, with dogs we need to catch their attention before we touch them, as otherwise we'd be displaying what they consider to be bad doggy manners and we could startle or frighten them. That isn't the response you would want to evoke in your dog!

'Every aspect of training your dog involves gaining and keeping his attention while you teach him how to figure out what you want from him and how he can achieve this.'

## Understanding words

Research has shown that dogs understand words that fit the vocabulary of a pre-school age child. Tests carried out with a Border collie called Chaser showed that she had a clear understanding of 1,022 words, and could retrieve many asked-for objects and discriminate between categories of objects as well as the objects themselves. Her training ceased at that point, so she may have been capable of understanding many more words if it had continued. This involves very complex thinking processes, and surely will increase your respect for your dog's potential learning abilities! But before your dog can understand specific words, you need to help him to create an association between the word and the object or action.

Here's a fun experiment you can try in order to see how challenging it is for your dog to decipher what you're asking of him before certain words become familiar. You'll need the help of a friend to do this. Stand facing each other and take it in turns to 'teach' each other – but the only words you can each use to give instructions are the names of fruits and vegetables. You can use body language, but no other words than these. Some of the instructions will be very hard to understand, because they're not in a context that you are familiar with. After repeatedly striving to communicate one point, you may find yourself raising your voice in the hope that this will make the true meaning clearer, or you may begin to feel giggly or frustrated. You may get bored with trying and want to walk away and do something else. This experiment is one way to gain an understanding into why your dog may find it difficult to follow your instructions at times, and why he gives up when he really can't figure out what you want. It's not because he's lacking in intelligence – it's a simple breakdown of communication due to the language barrier.

In the chapter 2 you discovered how to teach your dog to understand words such as 'sit', 'wait' and so on, and to follow through on these instructions. Your dog will be constantly learning throughout his life, guided by the feedback he receives from you. If he loses focus or finds something else more appealing than your company, you need to make your presence more inviting. The rule of thumb, as stated earlier, is always that dogs tend to repeat behaviours that they find in some way rewarding. This point can't be repeated too often, because it governs every action that your dog performs – whether he undertakes these independently or at your request.

So how can you train your dog to focus on you and concentrate on the message you're giving to him? You can teach him to observe your face. Dogs don't tend to do this with other dogs, because in their repertoire of 'good dog manners' it's actually very rude to look another dog directly in the eye. It can act as a prelude to confrontation and direct aggression. Yet a dog who has learned to trust you will happily gaze lovingly into your eyes, and a dog who doesn't know you well will try not to meet your eyes but will register the emotions which flit across your face.

'Before your dog can understand specific words, you need to help him to create an association between the word and the object or action.'

# Left gaze bias

Scientific studies at the University of Lincoln have shown that humans and dogs observe the right side of the face opposite them by sliding their gaze to the left. This is called 'left gaze bias'. For humans, this is an instinctive way of assessing the emotional state of a person. Dogs have also learned to use it as a way of gauging whether a human is safe to be around, but they don't do this with other dogs. Your dog uses left gaze bias to figure out whether you're pleased with him, whether he has your approval or disapproval, and whether he needs to beat a hasty retreat because you're feeling annoyed or angry.

Even just a brief glance at you reveals volumes to your dog. By teaching him to hold a focus on your face, you can keep his attention even in situations where he may be distracted, anxious or gearing up to race off and explore or play. The 'watch me' game is an easy way to gain your dog's attention on request.

# Watch me

Dogs love this training game because they swiftly realise how rewarding it is! You'll need a pocketful of treats for this, and you can speed up your dog's learning process if you use different treats to the usual ones. Small, wholesome dog treats such as pieces of dried liver, or tiny morsels of cheese, cooked chicken or thin slices of sausage are usually guaranteed to gain your dog's undivided attention.

Choose a time when your dog is relaxed. Between walk times and mealtimes is best, because your dog won't learn as easily if he's tired and he'll be less motivated by food rewards if he's just eaten. Practise the 'watch me' game indoors at first, away from too many distractions. When he seems to have 'got it', take him into the garden. Practise at home for a few days before using this during your walks, because you want to set your dog up for continued success.

'If he loses focus or finds something else more appealing than your company, you need to make your presence more inviting.'

Toes and Tara learn the 'watch me' signal

First of all, wait until your dog glances at you. Immediately say 'Watch me!' in a happy, excited voice and give him a treat as you say the phrase. Your dog will eat the treat and look expectantly at you in the hope of receiving more. As soon as he looks at your face, repeat the instruction and the reward. You need to be quick with this, so that he associates the phrase with looking at you and receiving a treat. You'll soon find that your dog's eyes are fixed firmly upon your face.

If your dog isn't looking at you, you can catch his attention by showing him a treat and holding it up in front of your eyes. As soon as his gaze follows the treat and he glances at you, say 'Watch me!' and reward him.

Once you feel you have your dog's full attention, walk backwards so that he can see your face while you move away. Adopt a happy, dancing step and smile, so that he knows you're pleased with him. He's likely to move towards you. As soon as he glances at your face, repeat 'Watch me!' and reward him. Step sideways and move around the room, encouraging him to stay close to you. After a while, walk beside him, going forward, so that he looks up at you as he accompanies you. Keep the phrase and rewards coming each time he glances up at your face. When you feel he's figured out what you want him to do, say 'Watch me!' when he looks away. If he responds instantly, reward him.

The next stage is to play this game in the garden, graduating to your usual walking areas only when you feel confident that he will respond to the phrase.

'Watch me' is an excellent way of helping your dog to calm down if he's overexcited and also helps him to cope if he experiences anxiety over the presence of other dogs. If your dog bounces around at the sight of other dogs or people, or reacts fearfully through shrinking back or lunging, using 'watch me' keeps his focus on you, instead of what's happening around him.

# Pointing

Fascinating studies into whether dogs and other mammals can solve problems by figuring out what we're thinking have been carried out at the Duke Canine Cognition Centre and the Max Planck Institute. One of these studies involved hiding treats beneath a cup and then pointing at the cup, to see whether dogs could work out what the researchers wanted them to do. The dogs 'got it' immediately and were rewarded with the treat inside each cup they knocked over. The research results showed that dogs are the only creatures, other than humans, who follow the trajectory of a pointing finger and go to investigate the area or object that we're pointing at.

You may have noticed that your dog tries to get your attention by using his nose to point at the area where his treats or toys are kept. He understands that this is a good way to show you what he wants. This is a behaviour that dogs have learned through observing us closely, and you can use your dog's predisposition for this silent form of communication by directing his attention, too.

If you want to teach your dog to retrieve a toy, to go to another person, or to focus on a specific object or area, you can do this by pointing and saying a chosen word – then rewarding him as soon as he follows through on your request. This can be a fun game for your dog and it increases the level of attention he pays to you.

'Research results showed that dogs are the only creatures, other than humans, who follow the trajectory of a pointing finger.'

# Summing Up

- During training it's important to gain, and maintain, your dog's attention.

- With dogs, we need to gain their attention before touching them.

- Your dog learns to understand words through creating associations between words and behaviours.

- If you imagine trying to make figure out the meaning of a language that makes no sense to you, this will help you understand why your dog sometimes gets confused.

- If your dog loses focus or gets bored, make yourself more interesting.

- Dogs use 'left gaze bias' to decipher our emotions and intentions.

- 'Watch me' is a fun game that ensures you have your dog's full attention.

- Teaching new lessons at home reduces the likelihood of distractions.

- Dogs can understand that when you point your finger, you want them to pay attention to something.

# Chapter Six

# Breed Skills

There are now over 400 registered dog breeds. Although domestic dogs have been part of our lives for at least 14,000 years, many of our Kennel Club recognised modern dog breeds emerged within the past 1,000 years – some as recently as within the last century. These have been deliberately engineered, through selective breeding, to carry out particular tasks or groups of tasks. The physical traits such as height, build, coat texture and colour, behaviour and aptitude to specific tasks all depend upon particular genes. Humans have been modifying these in dogs for a long time, by choosing and mating individuals from a desirable line in order to enhance certain physical characteristics.

## Different breeds

Dogs are grouped by breed into eight categories that are recognised by the Kennel Club. Some breeds, such as Yorkshire Terriers, may fit into more than one category. Then, of course, there are the mixed breeds, whose heritage may be either easily guessed at or indeterminate. The groups are: toy breeds, terrier breeds, sporting breeds, herding breeds, hound breeds, working dog breeds, non-sporting breeds and miscellaneous breeds. If your dog isn't mentioned in this chapter, you can look him up on the Kennel Club website to ascertain which group he fits into. Please bear in mind that new 'designer' mixes, such as Labradoodles (Labrador-Poodle) and Sprockers (Springer-Cocker Spaniel) aren't recognised by the Kennel Club, yet are considered to be breeds nowadays.

Your dog will have been bred to have specific skills, so you can use your understanding of his inherent gifts and predisposition to train him and select games which best suit his nature. It can be fun to figure out how you can

'Dogs are grouped by breed into eight categories that are recognised by the Kennel Club.'

stimulate the digging and hunting instincts of your Jack Russell Terrier while keeping your lawn intact, or to devise games for your Whippet or Greyhound that enable him to use his extraordinary visual abilities and speed.

## Toy breeds

Some of the very small dogs, such as Cavalier King Charles Spaniel, Chihuahua, Maltese Terrier, Papillon, Pekingese, Pomeranian, Pug and Shih-Tzu were bred as companions and lap dogs. They kept their owners warm whilst keeping them company. Others, such as the Affenpinscher, Italian Greyhound and Yorkshire Terrier were bred to hunt small game as well as for companionship.

'Dogs learn through play, so you can use games as part of your dog's training and bond more closely with him at the same time.'

If your dog is tiny, you may be more tempted to coddle, cuddle and pamper him than if he was a large dog, especially if he needs a lot of grooming. Many small breeds are treated as babies or toys by their owners, which doesn't do justice to their high levels of intelligence. Remember to allow your dog to be a dog! Small dogs tend to have a lot of energy. They live for longer than large breeds, and often they need more mental as well as physical stimulation.

Dogs learn through play, so you can use games as part of your dog's training and bond more closely with him at the same time. Chase the ball, find the treat or squeaky toy, mini obstacle or agility courses in your garden (or around your furniture) are all enjoyable for your dog and put more of a sparkle in his eye. As the toy breeds have been specifically bred to be companions, allow your dog plenty of opportunities for practising his social skills.

## Terrier breeds

All the terriers are included in this group. These range in size from the small Cairn Terriers, Jack Russell Terriers and West Highland Whites, to Fox Terriers, the larger and more compact Pitbulls and Staffordshire Bull Terriers and the tall, wiry Airedales. Terriers are a feisty, very courageous group of breeds, designed to hunt and kill rats, badgers, foxes and other creatures. It takes guts to go down into a dark tunnel and do battle with its inhabitant, and this strength of character is evident in the terrier personality.

Cyder digging

Terriers need plenty of physical exercise and mental stimulation. They're easily bored, and a bored dog can exhibit destructive tendencies. The smaller hunting breeds of terrier love to dig, and with some of these it may seem that gardening is a pointless pursuit. You need to set your fencing deep if you have a terrier, as they can dig their way under and go in search of more interesting activities than your garden provides.

Your terrier will thank you if you set aside a small area of your garden for him to go digging in. Hide treats or scented toys there, and encourage him to search for them. If he starts to dig elsewhere in the garden, calmly redirect him to his own area so that he learns that this is his special place. Some dedicated dog owners excavate and safely line underground tunnels for their terriers, or build wooden tunnels above ground, because the nature of the terrier is to burrow. You could use a children's play tunnel as an easy alternative.

Tracking games are fun for terriers. Lay a trail of treats that winds around and gets his nose interested and his paws moving. End the trail with a soft toy that he can throw around, giving full rein to his instinct to grab prey by the neck and shake it, or place a chew there for him to lie down and relax with. As terriers respond strongly to movement, you could attach a toy or treat to the end of a line and trail it around the garden for him to chase and catch.

## Sporting dog breeds

All the breeds of Spaniels, Labradors, Retrievers, Setters, Pointers and the Wirehaired Pointing Griffons come under this category. These high-energy working dogs need a lot of outdoor exercise, though they make good companions in the home, too, and are generally friendly with people outside their social group. Originally the Pointers were bred to sniff out game and to point it out to handlers, Spaniels to locate and flush (drive) fowl into the air, and Retrievers to retrieve fallen game from water or land without causing damage to it. Setters usually find, point and flush out game.

Sporting dogs pay a great deal of attention to instructions, as they work in partnership with their owners or handlers. This focus can make them easy to train, and they particularly enjoy pursuits that allow them to use their inherent skills. Their special talents can make them very suitable as service dogs.

Sporting dogs enjoy most activities that involve using plenty of energy. Fetch games and catch and return games are popular. Hide-and-seek, in which you hide a toy in bushes (or around the home) and direct your dog to locate and retrieve it, stimulate your sporting dog's natural abilities. Frisbee chasing and retrieving is fun for your dog, too. A soft Frisbee is preferable to a hard one that could damage your dog's mouth. If your dog enjoys water, you could set up a paddling pool for him, or play find and retrieve in a nearby shallow, slow-flowing stream. If he likes to dig, you could put a sandpit in your garden just for him to use.

## Herding dog breeds

Shepherds, Cattle dogs, Sheepdogs, Corgis and Bouvier des Flandres are just a few of the herding breeds. Although many are now bred to be family companions, originally these dogs were bred to herd sheep and cattle so have a great deal of energy and stamina. They're also highly intelligent, because their tasks include figuring out where the herd is going, how to manoeuvre individuals so that the herd or flock stays together, and how to gain and keep control of the herd. This instinct can be redirected onto family members if your dog doesn't have opportunities to use it appropriately, and one of the most common issues reported in herding breeds is their tendency to nip ankles as they work to gather family members together – whether or not you all want to be in the same space!

Agility classes are an ideal outlet for herding dog breeds, as these dogs love to run, jump and weave around. You can stimulate your herding dog by setting up obstacles for him to move in and out of, or get a small see-saw – you can

'Sporting dogs pay a great deal of attention to instructions, as they work in partnership with their owners or handlers. This focus can make them easy to train, and they particularly enjoy pursuits that allow them to use their inherent skills.'

make your own see-saw from a sturdy plank of wood balanced on a log, too. Flyball is an excellent game for herding breeds. Your dog will enjoy it if you scatter toys and ask him to collect and return them to you, especially if you teach him names for each toy and call those out so that he can locate them.

## Hound breeds

If your dog has 'hound' in his breed name, he'll be included in this group. This includes the sighthounds, such as Afghan Hounds, Deerhounds, Greyhounds, Borzois, Wolfhounds, Whippets and Salukis, and also Beagles, Foxhounds, Bassett Hounds and Rhodesian Ridgebacks, among others. These dogs were bred to hunt large and small game, and are built for either speed or stamina – in some, such as Wolfhounds and Salukis, for both of these qualities. Most of the sighthounds are sprinters; very fast, but they use their energy in short bursts and then need to rest. As their name suggests, they have keen sight and their prey drive is activated by movement. Basset Hounds rely on their sense of smell, and their long ears come in useful for wafting scents up to their noses. The other hound breeds have enduring stamina and can track prey over long distances.

'Agility classes are an ideal outlet for herding dog breed.'

Consider which of the senses your dog is most stimulated by when devising games for him. Bassets, Beagles and Foxhounds will thank you for laying scent trails for them to follow, with a prize buried or waiting at the end of the trail. You can make these as complex as you like, so that they curve around trees and bushes for maximum nose satisfaction.

Sighthounds love to run but often can't see the point of retrieving, so 'chase the ball or soft Frisbee' works particularly well for their movement-activated prey drive – although you may have to retrieve the object yourself when your dog has dropped it! You may also find there's a Greyhound playgroup in your area, where your dog can have fun socialising with his own kind.

## Working dog breeds

This group of dogs were bred to help humans with heavier work, and they're sturdy and strong. The working dog group includes Boxers, Akitas, Huskies, Alaskan Malamutes, Pyrenean and Bernese Mountain Dogs, Doberman

Pinschers, Portuguese Water Dogs, Newfoundlands, Schnauzers, Mastiffs and Leonbergers. These large breeds originally (and some still do) pull sledges and carts, carry out water and mountain rescues, and guard property. They have immense stamina and need an outlet for their inborn working natures.

Some areas have carting groups where owners bring their working dogs to have fun pulling carts or sledges. This enables your dog to take part in the task he was bred for, and also be part of a group – something that's important to some working breeds. Mountaineering or hiking with you, swimming, and even 'search and rescue' of objects gives your dog the stimulation he needs to keep him happy and healthy.

## Non-sporting breeds

'Consider which of the senses your dog is most stimulated by when devising games for him.'

This group is comprised of a variety of breeds which includes Boston and Tibetan Terriers, Chow Chows, Shar Peis, Lhasa Apso, Poodles, Bulldogs, Bichon Frises and Dalmations. Consider the games from other groups for these breeds, and choose the ones that you think your dog will enjoy. Perhaps a sandpit or digging area would make his day; or a paddling pool, sniffing trail or soft Frisbee.

## Mixed breeds

If your dog is a mixture of two or more breeds, figuring out his heritage by taking a close look at his appearance and interests will help you in finding the best outlets for his energy and intelligence. Mixed breeds tend, in general, to be healthier than pedigree dogs, because their gene pool is more diluted, and your mixed breed may be more energetic than his parents. Try out catch and retrieve games, scent games and chase games, and see which of these he likes best. Introduce him to water play and agility-type games such as see-saws and weaving in and out of objects. His wagging tail and eager expression will tell you which he enjoys most.

A dog who is well cared for, loved and allowed access to the physical and mental stimulation he needs is a happy, well-adjusted dog. Contented dogs respond most easily to training, so giving your dog plenty of opportunities to express his inner nature means that rewards are reaped for you, as well as for him.

# Summing Up

- There are now over 400 recognised modern dog breeds.

- Dogs are grouped by breed into eight categories by the Kennel Club.

- Small breeds often have a great deal more energy than large breeds.

- As dogs learn through play, you can incorporate games with training.

- Terriers need a lot of exercise and mental stimulation.

- Tracking games are fun for terriers and sporting dog breeds.

- Herding breeds often enjoy agility, Flyball and scatter and gather games.

- You can devise games that allow your dog to engage his primary sense.

- Dogs in the 'working' group were bred to assist humans with heavy tasks.

- Looking at the appearance and interests of your mixed breed will help you determine which games he'll most enjoy.

# Chapter Seven

# Fun and Games

Learning should always be fun and some 'tricks' can be very useful for helping your dog to be more relaxed in places such as the vets, where he may be anxious about the strange scents and having a stranger looming over him.

As with any teaching process, set a pace that is comfortable for your dog. If your dog doesn't seem to be 'getting it', you can break down each lesson into small increments, practising just one or two steps for a while before moving on to the next stage and rewarding him every time he figures out what you're asking of him.

## The name of the game

You won't find any 'tricks', such as dancing for human entertainment, in this chapter. The games you'll be teaching your dog here are all aimed at helping him behave calmly in different situations – and can also show others what a wonderful bond there is between you. In the case of 'fetch and deliver' you can even use this as a daily task, such as fetching the post or newspaper from the hallway, that makes your dog feel good about himself. Dogs were bred to be our helpmates and like to feel useful, and the dogs who misbehave are usually the ones who are bored and understimulated.

## Roll over

This is a great game for those times when your dog's underside needs to be thoroughly checked over by your vet. Learning to roll over onto his back involves trust on your dog's behalf, as you're teaching him to expose his

'As with any teaching process, set a pace that is comfortable for your dog.'

vulnerable throat and belly – something that he would normally only do when he's either very relaxed or when signalling submission in the face of a perceived threat.

Your dog will need to have learned to lie down before you teach him to roll over. You'll find the instructions for 'down' in chapter 2.

Ask him to lie down and then hold a treat to one side of his nose and eyes. As you move the treat upwards and sideways, his head and then his body will follow your hand. He'll start to slip sideways. Keep hold of the treat until his body reaches tipping point and rolls over. Immediately praise and reward him. Keep repeating the trick, saying 'Roll over' just as he rolls and you give him the treat. A gentle tummy rub will make him even happier to stay on his back for a few moments.

'Your dog will need to have learned to lie down before you teach him to roll over.'

Rosie learns 'roll over'

## Catch the ball

This game brings you and your dog together as a team. It's great for his coordination skills and he'll be very proud of himself when he learns how to play it! It's important to make sure the ball isn't small enough to get caught in his throat as he closes his teeth around it. A larger soft ball or rubber ball is ideal. Hard balls can damage your dog's mouth or teeth, so avoid these.

Maisie ball play

First play 'throw and retrieve'; with you throwing the ball and your dog bringing it back to you and dropping it at your feet or in your hand. This sets the scene for further cooperation. Next, throw the ball low, so that it's level with, or just above, his head. This makes it natural for your dog to catch it in his jaws. As soon as he manages to catch the ball, call 'Catch' in a gleeful tone of voice. Do a little victory dance, if you like – let your dog see you're really pleased with him. Call him to you and ask him to drop the ball, and then repeat the game, sending the ball higher as he becomes more expert at capturing it.

You'll find that, after a while, your dog will be in place to catch the ball even before you know its trajectory and landing place. It's as if he can predict where the ball will be. This is because your dog's eyes have a higher 'flicker-fusion rate' – his eyes can take more of the 'still snapshots' per second that make up moving images than your human eyes are capable of. Once he's mastered the 'catch' game, you can test this by trying to catch him out when you throw the ball – though it's guaranteed that most of the time he'll be the winner!

## Fetch and deliver

Even dogs who weren't bred to be retrievers enjoy bringing an object back to you, and the more rewards there are in this game, the faster he'll learn to play it. It gets him to pay attention to you while he figures out what you want him to retrieve, it makes him feel useful and it can, in fact, work as useful employment for a bright dog who may be easily bored. Remember to always praise and thank him and to give food rewards every time he gets it right, especially while you're teaching him.

Start off with a toy or a ball. Throw it for your dog and, as soon as he collects it, ask him to come to you. Use an excited tone of voice. He's likely to run up to you to find out what's so interesting. When he comes close, give him a treat and lots of praise.

Now throw the toy again, calling him as soon as he picks it up. As he moves towards you, say 'Fetch' in a happy, upbeat tone of voice, treating and praising him when he reaches you. The more you practise this, the faster he'll make the association that 'fetch' means you want him to bring the toy to you.

Once he has learned this game you can make it more complex. Place toys in a pile, or scatter them around, and ask him to 'tidy up' by bringing each one to you or placing it in a basket. You can also teach him to fetch his lead, your shoes, or any other objects.

## Give a paw

'In canine body language, dogs sometimes raise a paw if they're feeling uncertain or a little uncomfortable, so only teach your dog this game when he feels at ease with you.'

In canine body language, dogs sometimes raise a paw if they're feeling uncertain or a little uncomfortable, so only teach your dog this game when he feels at ease with you. It can be very useful when you need to check his paws or nails, or if he's muddy and you need to clean him up. Some dogs are sensitive about having their paws touched, so this game can help them overcome this.

Skye 'giving paw'

Make sure your dog is in a relaxed state, perhaps a few minutes after a game when he's wound down from an excited state but isn't sleepy. Call him over to you and ask him to 'sit'. Hold a treat up in front of his nose and gently touch his paw. His paw may rise naturally. If it doesn't, gently take his paw in your hand as you give him the treat. Repeat this several times, saying 'Give a paw' or 'Shake hands'. Gently place his paw back on the ground afterwards and reward him again. He'll soon figure out that you're asking him to place his paw in your hand.

Some dogs start to expect to be given a reward each time they offer a paw, unasked, and can get into the bad habit of pawing at you in the expectation of treats on demand. If your dog does this, turning away without giving the dual rewards of a treat and your attention will soon nip this habit in the bud.

### Speak!

In chapter 2 you learned how to teach your dog to stop barking. You can also teach him to 'speak' on request. As well as this being a good communication game between you and your dog, this can also be useful if you're not sure who is there when your doorbell rings.

It's best to teach this after your dog has learned to be quiet at your request, so that he knows to bark when asked, instead of at random.

Wait until your dog barks at something. As soon as he starts barking, say 'Speak!' in a happy tone of voice. Reward him with a treat and praise. If he barks again, say 'Speak!' and reward him. Repeat this each time he gives a woof. When you're ready, ask him to 'Stop' and reward him for stopping.

At first you'll need to have a few treats in your pocket all the time, so that you can teach him to 'Speak!' every time he begins to bark, and subsequently ask him to 'Stop' if he carries on for too long or becomes overexcited. After a while, though, he'll understand what you want him to do when you say the word.

## How to set up your own agility or obstacle course

Dogs enjoy interesting activities, and you can find out more about training classes and agility classes in the next chapter. If you create an agility or obstacle course in your garden, this gives him mental as well as physical exercise and helps keep him flexible, fit and youthful. You don't need a large garden for this and you can custom design your course to fit your dog's energy level, agility and strength.

Young dogs, especially large breeds, shouldn't jump up or down from a height equivalent to getting into a car boot, because it puts too much pressure on the joints and bones and can cause health issues later on. They shouldn't turn sharply, for the same reasons. Older dogs with stiff joints or health issues shouldn't be challenged in this way, either, so tailor your course to suit your dog's age and state of health.

'If you create an agility or obstacle course in your garden, this gives him mental as well as physical exercise and helps keep him flexible, fit and youthful. Tailor your course to suit your dog's age and state of health.'

You can buy ready-made dog agility sets from stores such as Amazon, and you'll find a selection of inexpensive equipment at Pets at Home, but you may prefer to make your own. Your agility or obstacle course could include: a line of sticks or poles set into the ground for him to weave in and out of (bamboo canes from your local garden centre work well); a see-saw (you can make your own using a sturdy plank of wood balanced on a log); a child's play tunnel for your dog to run through; a hula hoop that you can fix in place or hold up for your dog to jump through; a plank of wood fixed on two blocks for your dog to run along; and a sturdy wooden box for your dog to stay still on for a moment.

## Patience and reward

It's best to use food rewards to lure your dog through the course until he figures out what you want him to do at each obstacle. Once he's 'got it' he'll be keen to race around simply for fun, though it's good to reward him with lots of praise while he's negotiating his way through and when he completes the course.

Hold a treat between your thumb and forefinger and run slightly ahead of your dog so that he can see the treat and also see where you're heading. He'll follow your hand, so use this to direct him through and over the obstacles. With the tunnel, go to the beginning, then run to the far end and show him the treat so that he runs into the tunnel and gets the reward at the far side.

Be patient if he takes a while to figure out what you want him to do, and avoid trying to coerce him if he doesn't want to do something – try again another day. Reward him with praise and a treat after each object has been successfully negotiated.

# Summing Up

■ Breaking down each lesson into small increments can help him learn more easily.

■ Games such as 'roll over' can be useful when your dog needs a vet check.

■ Playing 'catch the ball' encourages teamwork.

■ Your dog can predict where an object will land much more accurately than you can.

■ Bringing objects to you on request helps your dog to feel useful.

■ Teach your dog when he's in a relaxed state of mind.

■ Once you've taught your dog to stop barking on request, you can teach him to 'speak' to you.

■ An agility or obstacle course keeps your dog's mind and body fitter and more flexible.

# Chapter Eight

# Training and Agility Classes

Training and agility classes which employ positive, reward-based methods provide good opportunities for your dog to develop his social skills and to learn the appropriate responses to new instructions. As they should be enjoyable for both you and your dog, it's important to check out the classes in your area before enrolling so that you can decide which one best suits you. You'll find useful contact details in the help list towards the end of this book. First check whether the trainer is qualified and is a member of a reputable training organisation. Ask the instructor whether you can visit and observe a class, without your dog, in order to make up your mind whether this group will be right for him and you. If the instructor doesn't allow you to do this, remove that class from your list of potentials, as a good trainer should be willing for you to watch him or her at work.

## Training classes

Dog training classes show you how you can teach your dog to follow specific instructions and requests. The levels of complexity vary from puppy socialisation classes, which allow pups to spend time with other young dogs and usually to learn the basics such as 'sit', 'stay' and 'lie down', to adult dog training classes for beginner, intermediate and advanced training.

'Training and agility classes which employ positive, reward-based methods provide good opportunities for your dog to develop his social skills and to learn the appropriate responses to new instructions.'

# Agility classes

Agility classes are excellent for very energetic dogs and bright dogs who are easily bored. A class may have up to twenty different obstacles for your dog to go over, around, through and under as they negotiate the course. If the class enters dogs for competitions, the dogs will be timed as they move through the course and points may be awarded for how your dog deals with each obstacle or piece of equipment. There are tailor-made agility courses for all ages of dogs, but puppies and older or stiff-jointed dogs shouldn't be subjected to anything involving jumping or fast turns that could adversely affect their health. Agility can be done just for fun or taken seriously at competition level.

Bear in mind that you'll be running around the course with your dog, so you'll need plenty of energy and stamina – it's an agility class for you, too! If you enjoy being active this is a great way for both of you to stay fit.

'Agility can be done just for fun or taken seriously at competition level.'

# Class considerations

With a training or agility class, the main points to take into consideration are the approach of the trainer, the number of dogs attending, the space, the resources available and the atmosphere around the dogs and their owners.

## Trainers

Trainers who use positive reinforcement and reward-based methods are usually very happy to discuss these with you even before you attend the class. This will be a strong indication that this class operates along the right lines for you and your dog. Unfortunately, some trainers still use and recommend harsh dominance methods and unsavoury disciplinary 'training aids' such as yanking on the lead, shouting, check/choke chains, prong collars, electric collars and noise-making devices that are aimed at shocking dogs into submission. You wouldn't want your dog to be subjected to any of these.

## Number of pupils!

A small number of dogs (preferably no more than six) usually work best. The larger the group, the easier it becomes for a dog to feel intimidated or overwhelmed and for the class to spiral out of control. A trainer can only focus on a few dogs at a time so, if the group is large, shifts in body language that show a dog is becoming anxious or stressed are less likely to be noticed before his behaviour starts to escalate.

## Size and space

Look at the size of the training space in relation to the number of dogs and owners present. Is it confined, with only a few inches between each dog? Or is there plenty of room for the dogs and owners to manoeuvre without bumping into each other? If the space seems cramped, the dogs are more likely to focus on each other instead of their owner's guidance. This makes for too many distractions and your dog will find it much harder to learn what you're teaching him. Plenty of space between dogs will help to keep your dog from becoming anxious or overexcited, and will make it much easier for you to gain his attention. Does the class consist mostly of disruptive or hyper-energetic dogs, rather than simply untrained dogs? If so, this won't be helpful for your dog.

'Ask yourself whether the dogs and their owners seem generally happy and relaxed.'

## Equipment

With agility classes, check out the equipment, too. Is it in good condition? If a dog seems anxious about using any of the equipment, is the leader of the class patient and understanding? If force, coercion or disapproval is used on any of the dogs, it's best to look for another class.

## Atmosphere and mood

Get a 'feel' for the atmosphere at the class. Ask yourself whether the dogs and their owners seem generally happy and relaxed. Are they clearly enjoying the class, or do they seem anxious? Are any of the dogs particularly disruptive or unruly, or cowed and nervous? If the majority of the dogs seem ill at ease, this won't be the class for you. Sometimes the owner of a fear-reactive, timid or nervous dog will take him to a class to help him gain confidence. If you notice a noisy or scared-looking dog in the class, observe the trainer's attitude towards dog and owner. A good trainer will be calmly reassuring and in control. He or she will ensure that a nervous or reactive dog has extra space around him so that he feels safer.

Another point to look for is whether the dogs have an opportunity to socialise and play at some point during the class. As the main reasons for attending are to encourage the development of good social skills and to learn required responses to training in a group situation, there should be some play as well as work – and the training itself should be fun.

# Summing Up

- Dog training classes show you how to teach your dog to follow instructions.

- Agility classes use equipment that provides mental and physical stimulation.

- You'll be expending a lot of energy alongside your dog in agility classes.

- Ensure your trainer is qualified and registered with an appropriate organisation.

- Check that only positive, reward-based methods are used in the classes.

- Avoid classes that use harsh disciplinary 'training aids'.

- A small group is far better than a large one.

- It's important that dogs have space around them in training classes.

- A happy atmosphere, where dogs and owners are enjoying the class, is important.

- The inclusion of a play-break helps to develop your dog's social skills.

- Training or agility classes should be enjoyable for you and your dog.

# Chapter Nine

# More Dogs, More Fun

The sight of several dogs enjoying each other's company is delightful. Dogs are social creatures and enjoy sniffing around and playing tag with other familiar dogs who they feel safe around. If you have two or more dogs, or if your dog has a few canine friends, it can be fun for them to engage in group activities and games. The following suggestions all provide mental, as well as physical, stimulation, and some games reinforce the training they have already learned. Keep the games short (ten minutes of each is plenty) so that the dogs don't become either bored or hyper, but give them plenty of time for indulging in sniffing and water games. If a dog gets overexcited, stop play immediately, before it spins out of control.

If any of the dogs chooses not to join in, allow them to rest or do their own thing. The object of group activities is for the dogs to enjoy themselves, so avoid any temptation to persuade a reluctant dog to take part.

'The best play places for a group of dogs are a garden or field.'

## Playtime!

The best play places for a group of dogs are a garden or field. With garden 'water play' you could use a hose, sprinkler or paddling pool. Beyond the home, the opportunity to run around at the beach or a safe stream is usually very popular with dogs, too. Encourage cooperation and interaction between dogs during group activities. A little competition in games such a 'speed-sit' is fine, but you'll want to avoid the risk of any of the dogs becoming irritable if he sees all the rewards going to another dog, so aim for fairness.

## Water play

Most dogs enjoy water. If the weather's warm, set up a sprinkler in your garden and run through it so that the dogs follow. They'll soon be dashing in and out while you watch from the sidelines. Put a few inches of water in a sturdy paddling pool (the type with solid sides is preferable to an inflatable pool that could be punctured), throw in some toys or treats for the dogs to go after and watch the fun. Trips to a dog-friendly beach or a slow-flowing stream give your dog lots of sniffing opportunities as well as water play.

## Football

'Trips to a dog-friendly beach or a slow-flowing stream give your dog lots of sniffing opportunities as well as water play.'

You'll be the leader in this game. If other people are taking part you could use more than one football for maximum fun. Ask the dogs to 'sit'. Kick the ball into the air, saying 'Go' as you do so. Let the dogs chase the ball and play with it for a minute or two. Ask the dog who has the ball to bring it back to you so that you can start over with the game.

## Relay game

The 'relay game' is a variation on Flyball relays. You can make it a speed competition, but it's nicer to just play it for fun. You can play this with any number of dogs and one or two teams. If you have one team, you'll need two people. Two teams need three people. This game requires 'prizes' of two soft balls or fluffy toys. If you have two teams, divide the dogs and match them up so that there's an even mix of faster and slower dogs in each team. A person needs to stay beside each team, while the extra person (the leader) stands centrally at least ten feet in front of both teams, holding the balls or toys.

Ask the dogs to 'sit' – in a line, if possible, but otherwise they can sit close together. The person ahead calls out the name of one dog and you send that dog to collect the toy and bring it back to your team. Praise and reward him as you ask him to drop the toy. Give the toy to the next dog as the team leader calls his name, so that he returns it to the leader. The leader asks for the toy and rewards that dog before sending him back to his team. The next dog to be called goes to collect the toy – and so on.

This game is great for teaching impulse control, as the dogs' natural reaction will be to dash forward as a group and they need to wait until it is their turn. It's also very good for extra tuition in recall in a group situation. Remember to praise and reward all the dogs when the game is over!

## Treasure hunt

Dogs thoroughly enjoy this game. It provides plenty of olfactory stimulation and gives them exercise at the same time.

Lay several overlapping trails of tiny treats that wind around the garden or field, around plants, bushes and trees if you have those. The dogs can watch you the first time, as long as they wait, but on subsequent plays you can let them figure it out for themselves.

Tell the dogs to 'Go find' and watch them sniff around, looking for treats to snaffle up.

## Treasure hunt with socks

This game works even better if the socks are unwashed, because the scent is very appealing to dogs! You'll need small treats and a sock for each dog.

Allow each dog to sniff the socks before the game begins. Lay a treasure hunt trail, as you did for the previous game. Hide a sock at the end of each trail. Send the dogs off to follow the treat trail. When all the socks have been found (some dogs may end up finding more than one), ask the dogs to return them to you. Praise and reward them when they do so.

## Speed-sit

Call the group of dogs over to you then ask them to 'sit'. Give a treat to each dog in the order that he 'sat' in. Repeat as often as you like.

## Down and race to owner

Call the dogs to you and ask them to lie down. Step several feet away and call each dog to you by name. If a dog becomes too enthusiastic and comes before he's called, take him back to the starting point and ask him to lie down again. Each dog receives praise and reward as he arrives by your side, and is then sent off to play.

## Rover says . . .

Gather the dogs together and take them through their repertoire of training at speed, asking them to sit, lie down, stay and come as a group. This can be useful for reinforcing training, as the dogs pay attention to each other as well as to you. Reward all of them afterwards.

# Summing Up

- Dogs enjoy playing with other friendly dogs.
-  Garden or field is ideal for group games.
- A water sprinkler or paddling pool provide lots of fun.
- Capitalise on your dog's enjoyment of ball games.
- Relay games are good for teaching impulse control.
- Treasure hunt games give opportunities for indulging the sense of smell.
- You can use games as extra reinforcement for training.

# Chapter Ten

# Additional Information

This book has taken you through the basics of teaching your dog how to exhibit behaviours and responses that make him a well-mannered, well-rounded companion who is a pleasure to have around. Your relationship will be smoother and happier through knowing that you and your dog can communicate effectively with each other. This chapter explores some additional ways in which you can make the most of the bond with him.

## Communication

### Hand signals

Hand signals can be especially useful for those times when you're some distance from your dog. They're also invaluable for clear communication with hard of hearing or deaf dogs. You'll find that you soon start to use some of the hand signals automatically, as you learned these in chapter 2. Here's a brief reminder of them.

#### Sit

Hold your hand in front of your dog (you can place your thumb and forefinger together, as if giving a treat, if you like) and raise your wrist slightly so that it looks as if you're about to give him a treat.

#### Down

Lower your hand towards the floor with your palm facing downwards.

'Your relationship will be smoother and happier through knowing that you and your dog can communicate effectively with each other.'

### Come

Pat your thigh or chest area.

### Stay and stop

Hold your hand out in front of you with your palm out, like a traffic cop.

### Watch me

Raise your hand to your eyes or the side of your face at eye level, with your thumb and forefinger together as if you're holding a treat.

### Off

Point your forefinger to the area where you want your dog to move to.

## A harness versus a lead

'When a dog wearing a collar and lead suddenly leaps forward, an enormous amount of stress and pressure is put on his delicate throat and neck.'

The common practice of walking dogs with a lead attached to the collar works fine for dogs who already stay close to the owner, but if your dog is learning to walk nicely on-lead, or is a puller, a good, well-fitting padded harness is much better for him and far easier for you.

When a dog wearing a collar and lead suddenly leaps forward, an enormous amount of stress and pressure is put on his delicate throat and neck. This can cause a great deal of discomfort and even serious injuries or health issues. If your dog lunges forward when he sees another dog, he's likely to associate other dogs with the pain that is caused by the sudden jerking of his lead and this can spark off potential issues such as fear-aggression. At the same time, you are jerked off balance, which can make you prone to painful muscular injuries. A good harness keeps you and your dog safe and more comfortable, but the anti-pull harnesses which cause discomfort to your dog should be avoided.

Some people find harnesses difficult to put on – especially if you have to figure out which way up they should be before raising your dog's legs to get them in the harness. The best harnesses are the Perfect Fit style ones which go over the head and fasten around the girth (see the help list). You can ask for a D ring (where the lead clips on) to be added to the chest area as well as on the back section if your dog is a puller. Initially you'll need to clip a lead to each D ring so that your dog finds himself turning slightly sideways instead of forging ahead when he pulls, but you'll soon find that you only need one lead clipped to the back D ring.

A well-fitted harness will make walks more comfortable for you and your dog, and will make it much easier for you to teach him to walk without pulling.

## Clicker training

This excellent method works through using a small hand-held device called a 'clicker' to *mark* and reinforce a desired behaviour. The short, sharp 'click' sound must be followed immediately (within one second) by a reward, because the sound of the clicker tells your dog he has done something right and the reward fixes this response in his mind.

Initially food rewards are used, so that your dog quickly learns to pay attention when he hears the 'click' sound. Once your dog is familiar with the clicker, and responsive to it, you can substitute other forms of reward, such as a toy or game. Eventually just the sound of the 'click' acts as a reward for your dog.

For instance, to use clicker training to teach your dog to 'sit', you just 'click' the moment he sits of his own accord, rewarding him immediately with a tasty treat. Follow this through every time he sits, adding your vocal cue of 'Sit' as you 'click'. After a while you can tell him to 'Sit' and mark his response to your instruction with the clicker and a treat the moment he follows through on the instruction.

Because the 'click' and reward need to be instant, you may want to practise on your own first. Try dropping something and 'clicking' the moment it touches the floor, then when you've mastered an accurate response, start using the clicker with your dog.

'A well-fitted harness will make walks more comfortable for you and your dog, and will make it much easier for you to teach him to walk without pulling.'

# Set up a dog-walking group or fun day

In chapter 9 you read about games you can play with a group of dogs. It can also enhance your dog's social life (and skills) if you get together with other dog people in your area and arrange regular group walks through a dog-friendly park or beach, or in nearby countryside. These give you the opportunity to make new friends with a common interest, too!

You could set this up by chatting with people you meet on your walks and arranging a time that's convenient for all of you to get together. Or, if you don't see many other people while you're out, a small advert in the local newspaper can work well.

It's best if all the dogs have already developed social skills around other dogs, because it will spoil the walk if you have to step in should a fight break out. Keep all the dogs on-lead at first, until you feel confident that they will get on well together. It's a good opportunity for practising loose-lead walking and calm introductions! When it feels right to let the dogs run and play, do this in a small group initially, a few dogs at a time, so that the more nervous or shy dogs don't feel overwhelmed.

Dog fun days are always popular. You could arrange one in aid of your favourite dog rescue charity, or for another charity in your area. Ideas could include a home-made agility course and informal dog show, as well as the games in chapter 9. Events in a fun dog show could be best-behaved dog, waggiest tail, most appealing puppy and elderly dog, best condition, dog most like his owner – ask around and your friends will be able to add to your list of events.

# Be a responsible dog owner

Your role as the carer of your dog is to keep him safe, well-nourished, sheltered, comfortable and in good physical, mental and emotional health. You also have a responsibility to make sure that other people and dogs are safe around your dog and to clean up after your dog, especially in public places. Legally, you are required to have an ID tag with your name, address and phone number attached to your dog's collar and to ensure that your dog is kept on-lead in areas where there are livestock.

Dog behaviour specialist Dr Jez Rose set up the National Responsible Dog Owners Campaign with the aim of making life safer and more enjoyable for dog owners, dogs and the general public. You can find out all about this on the dedicated website at www.nationaldogcampaign.co.uk.

Statistics reveal that 23% of households in the United Kingdom have at least one dog, with a total dog population of around 8 million. Studies have repeatedly shown that many owners experience increased feelings of emotional wellbeing and even improved physical health, thanks to the companionship and affection they receive from their dogs.

Our four-legged friends easily become much-loved family members. The dog is said to be Man's best friend, which isn't surprising when you consider he has been our closest companion and helper for many thousands of years. By taking steps to understand your dog, to respect his innate doggy nature and to teach him acceptable, desirable ways of behaving, you are ensuring that this very special friendship becomes even closer.

'Your role as the carer of your dog is to keep him safe, well-nourished, sheltered, comfortable and in good physical, mental and emotional health.'

# Summing Up

- Hand signals can be very useful if your dog is further away, or is hard of hearing.

- A well-fitted harness is better than a collar and lead.

- Clicker training uses a small device that marks desired behaviour with a clicking sound.

- A dog-walking group or fun day enhances your social life, as well as your dog's.

- It's important to observe the codes of responsible dog ownership.

- Our dogs are family members as well as four-legged friends.

# Glossary

### Calming signals
A term first coined by Norwegian dog trainer Turid Rugaas. When dogs are stressed they use appeasing body language which includes a number of signals such as lip-licking, yawning and head-turning, to show that their intentions are peaceful.

### Conditioning – classical
Also called respondent conditioning. This is a way of influencing behaviour which involves eliciting a predictable response that the dog has no control over. An example is Pavlov's dogs, who salivated on hearing a bell because they had previously been given food when a bell rang.

### Conditioning – operant
Also called instrumental conditioning. If a dog is rewarded (deliberately or inadvertently) while exhibiting a behaviour, he will repeat that behaviour. This conditioning is used in positive dog training. A reward is consistently given as soon as the dog follows or performs a desirable behaviour. Over time this behaviour becomes automatic, whether or not a reward is given.

### Dominance
The old, scientifically disproved methods of dog training were based on the erroneous theory that dogs wanted to be dominant 'alphas' over humans and other creatures. The dominance method involves intimidating dogs into submission by showing forcefully that the human is 'boss'. This theory has caused a great deal of unnecessary stress and suffering to dogs and humans, and has no place in positive methods of dog training.

### Extinguishing
This is a method by which you permanently stop an unwanted behaviour from recurring, through ensuring that the dog ceases to find that behaviour rewarding in any way.

### Fear-aggression

This is an aggressive reaction, such as barking, lunging, growling, snarling or biting, which occurs because the dog is afraid and feels there is no alternative but to react strongly.

### Negative reinforcement

This is a method in which the trainer aims to stop unwanted behaviour by making the dog feel uncomfortable while he displays that behaviour. An example is jerking on the dog's lead when he pulls or lunges. This method isn't used in positive dog training, as it goes against the principle of eliciting the dog's willing cooperation.

### Oxytocin

Also called the 'love hormone'. Oxytocin floods the system during moments of affectionate emotional connection, such as soft eye contact and stroking.

### Positive reinforcement

This is the act of rewarding desirable or requested behaviour *as soon* as it occurs. This sets up a pleasant association between action and reward, and helps the dog to learn more effectively.

### Recall

Calling the dog back to his owner.

### Redirection

The act of offering an alternative focus or activity that distracts the dog towards something he will perceive as more rewarding when he is carrying out an unwanted behaviour.

### Training

The process of teaching your dog to respond to your requests or instructions.

# Help List

## The APBC (Association of Pet Behaviour Counsellors)

www.apbc.org.uk
Tel: 01386 751151
Email: info@apbc.org.uk
A network of behaviourists offering help and advice. Their counsellors have achieved the highest proven academic and practical standards available in the field of companion behavioural therapy.

## Battersea Dogs & Cats Home

www.battersea.org.uk
Tel: 0843 509 4444
Well-known rescue home that takes in dogs (and cats) and attempts to reunite them with their owners or rehome them.

## Dog-Games Shop

www.dog-games-shop.co.uk
Tel: 01684 569553
Email: info@dog-games.co.uk
Recommended by vets and rescue centres, you can purchase the Perfect Fit Harness amongst other things here.

## The Dog Helpine

www.thedoghelpline.com
Email: thedoghelpline@gmail.com
Provides advice via Skype and over the telephone for any concerns you may have about your dog.

# Dogs Trust

www.dogstrust.org.uk

Tel: 0207 837 0006

The UK's largest dog welfare charity, providing care, rehoming and information on legislation and campaigning. There are 18 Dogs Trust Rehoming Centres around the UK.

# ISCP (International School of Canine Psychology)

www.theiscp.com

Provides globally approved diploma courses and workshops in dog behaviour.

# INTO Dogs

www.intodogs.org

The Association of Intuitive Natural Training for Owners is an organisation for qualified trainers and behaviourists who use only positive methods. You can contact them to ask for details of members in your area. INTO Dogs also has a cybercafé that's open to the public. You can browse through the areas of interest, or post questions about your dog and receive advice from qualified behaviorists and trainers.

# Dr Jez Rose (Canine Behavioural Specialist)

www.thebehaviourcompany.com

Tel: 0800 8600 156

This website has useful free tips about dog behaviour.

# Oldies Club Dog Rescue

www.oldies.org.uk

Oldies Club is an independent charity which takes in dogs over the age of 7. The dogs are assessed in foster homes before going to their new 'forever' homes. Often the reason for rehoming is because of the ill-health or bereavement of their previous owner.

# Pet Dog Trainers of Europe

www.pdte.org
This organisation has members throughout Europe and the UK, and uses only positive training methods. Some of the members run training classes.

# Responsible Dog Owners Campaign

www.nationaldogcampaign.co.uk
Founded by Dr Jez Rose, the campaign aims to help people better understand canine behaviour, to make owning and living with dogs safer and more enjoyable for both owners and the general public.

# RSPCA

www.rspca.org.uk
The leading UK animal welfare charity. Contact them for information on rehoming a dog, or advice on caring for your dog and how to report suspected mistreatment of animals.

# Three Counties Dog Rescue

www.threecountiesdogrescue.org
Tel: 07708 589 792 or 07718 269 191
Email: info@threecountiesdogrescue.org
A popular local (to the Need2Know publishing offices) independently run rescue centre for cats and dogs. Also offers resources for dog training and contacts to recommended dog behaviourists. Three Counties never puts animals to sleep for behavioural problems, and has many volunteers specially trained to work with dogs to improve their chances of being rehomed or placed into foster care.

# BOOK LIST

Bradshaw, John. *In Defence of Dogs: Why Dogs Need Our Understanding*. Allen Lane

Clothier, Suzanne. *Bones Would Rain from the Sky: Deepening Our Relationships with Dogs*. Warner Books

Coppinger, Raymond and Lorna. Dogs: *A New Understanding of Canine Origin, Behavior and Evolution*. Crosskeys

Coren, Stanley. *How to Speak Dog*. Pocket Books

Donaldson, Jean. *The Culture Clash*. James & Kenneth

Eaton, Barry. *Dominance: Fact or Fiction?* Dogwise

Horowitz, Alexandra. *Inside of a Dog: What Dogs See, Smell and Know*. Simon and Schuster

Lowry, Rosie and Aspinall, Marilyn. *Understanding the Silent Communication of Dogs*. Lowry Industries Ltd

McGreevy, Paul. *The Modern Dog's Life: How to Do the Best for Your Dog*.

Rugaas, Turid. *On Talking Terms with Dogs*. Qanuk

Rugaas, Turid. *My Dog Pulls. What Do I Do?* Dogwise

Spiers, Winkie. *How to Handle Living with Your Dog*. Short Stack Publishing

Tenzin-Dolma, Lisa. *Adopting a Rescue Dog*. Phoenix Rising Press

Tenzin-Dolma, Lisa. *The Heartbeat at Your Feet: A Practical, Compassionate New Way to Train Your Dog*. Rowman & Littlefield

Thompson, Jenifer. *Caring For Your Dog: The Essential Guide*. Need2Know Books

# References

Studies into dog cognition by Dr Alexandra Horowitz and her team, which include whether dogs feel guilt, can be found at: http://www.columbia.edu/~ah2240/

A University of Lincoln scientific paper about left gaze bias in humans, rhesus monkeys and domestic dogs can be downloaded at: http://eprints.lincoln.ac.uk/2423/

The statistics for the UK dog population are at: http://www.pfma.org.uk/pet-population/

# Need - 2 - Know

## Available Titles Include ...

**Allergies** A Parent's Guide
ISBN 978-1-86144-064-8 £8.99

**Autism** A Parent's Guide
ISBN 978-1-86144-069-3 £8.99

**Blood Pressure** The Essential Guide
ISBN 978-1-86144-067-9 £8.99

**Dyslexia and Other Learning Difficulties**
A Parent's Guide ISBN 978-1-86144-042-6 £8.99

**Bullying** A Parent's Guide
ISBN 978-1-86144-044-0 £8.99

**Epilepsy** The Essential Guide
ISBN 978-1-86144-063-1 £8.99

**Your First Pregnancy** The Essential Guide
ISBN 978-1-86144-066-2 £8.99

**Gap Years** The Essential Guide
ISBN 978-1-86144-079-2 £8.99

**Secondary School** A Parent's Guide
ISBN 978-1-86144-093-8 £9.99

**Primary School** A Parent's Guide
ISBN 978-1-86144-088-4 £9.99

**Applying to University** The Essential Guide
ISBN 978-1-86144-052-5 £8.99

**ADHD** The Essential Guide
ISBN 978-1-86144-060-0 £8.99

**Student Cookbook – Healthy Eating** The Essential Guide
ISBN 978-1-86144-069-3 £8.99

**Multiple Sclerosis** The Essential Guide
ISBN 978-1-86144-086-0 £8.99

**Coeliac Disease** The Essential Guide
ISBN 978-1-86144-087-7 £9.99

**Special Educational Needs** A Parent's Guide
ISBN 978-1-86144-116-4 £9.99

**The Pill** An Essential Guide
ISBN 978-1-86144-058-7 £8.99

**University** A Survival Guide
ISBN 978-1-86144-072-3 £8.99

View the full range at **www.need2knowbooks.co.uk**.
To order our titles call **01733 898103**, email **sales@ n2kbooks.com** or visit the website. Selected ebooks available online.

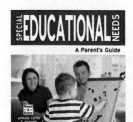

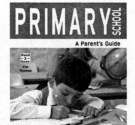
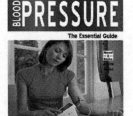
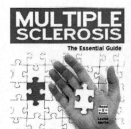

**Need - 2 - Know**, Remus House, Coltsfoot Drive, Peterborough, PE2 9BF